JOY COMES IN THE
MOURNING

Tabitha Joy Price

JOY COMES IN THE
MOURNING

TATE PUBLISHING
AND ENTERPRISES, LLC

Published by Tate Publishing & Enterprises, LLC

127 E. Trade Center Terrace | Mustang, Oklahoma 73064 USA
1.888.361.9473 | www.tatepublishing.com

Tate Publishing is committed to excellence in the publishing industry. The company reflects the philosophy established by the founders, based on Psalm 68:11,

"The Lord gave the word and great was the company of those who published it."

Book design copyright © 2012 by Tate Publishing, LLC. All rights reserved.
Cover design by Joel Uber
Interior design by Ronnel Luspoc

Published in the United States of America

ISBN: 978-1-62024-499-9
1. Biography & Autobiography / Personal Memoirs
2. Religion / Christian Life / Spiritual Growth
12.09.28

ENDORSEMENTS

"This book should be required reading for every Christian leader. No longer can we bury our heads in the sand and shun Christians who make wrong choices. With vulnerability, honesty, and painful truth-telling, Tabitha Price has given us a resource that helps us to choose a biblical response when a fellow Christian falls. This book reveals the power of forgiveness, the strength of Christian compassion, and the unmistakable road to joy after betrayal. Don't miss it."

—Carol Kent, speaker and author
When I Lay My Isaac Down (NavPress)
Between a Rock and a Grace Place (Zondervan)

"This is an agonizing and compelling account--of the sin and shame that could be ours, of the love and loyalty that comes with faith, and of the depth and spiritual maturity that only comes with brokenness. Read this book as warning and as inspiration. I found it to be a profoundly impactful testimony that glorifies God and stirs the reader toward the upward call."

—Dr. Joel C. Hunter, Senior Pastor
Northland – A Church Distributed

DEDICATION

To my precious soul mate, Joel.
You, have I loved, from childhood.

ACKNOWLEDGMENTS

Some might imagine that writing this book has alleviated my suffering. Those who know me best and have stood by me through this process know otherwise. Rather, writing this book has been cathartic in the same way that cauterizing a wound might be. Truly my family and friends have supported me richly as I have written this book, and a simple acknowledgement will never suffice for all I owe them.

Thank you, Dar Gail, my precious sister and friend, for your willingness to face the pain with me, for the hours of proofreading and editing, for the heartfelt prayers and constant flow of fresh ideas. As the older sister, I have always seen it as my privilege to look after you, but you have looked after me in so many ways during my darkest hours. I will never be able to express how much that means to me. Mom and Dad, you have always modeled for me what it means to live what you believe. Thank you for raising me to know and love God. It has made all the difference in this journey. Mom and Dad Price, your prayers and active role in our current "normal" have kept me going. Thank you for the mountain of support you have been to both Joel and me. Tammy, I know reading this book brought fresh waves of pain for you. We are so close that my pain truly is yours. Thank you for bearing this sorrow with me and for loving Joel like a brother. Though we were born eighteen months apart, in mind and heart we are truly twins. Jan, God has bound us together in a unique way, and I cannot thank Him enough for your powerful input into my life. You speak grace and love into our family every time we are together. Your faithful reading of each chapter and constant encouragement kept me writing more. Marshall, Jaden, and Roman, you teach me more than you will ever know. In this life, no matter what comes my way, I know I am truly blessed to call you my own, precious children. Thank you for walking this path with childlike trust.

Most of all, thank You, Jesus. For You and You alone, give joy in the mourning.

CONTENTS

JOY COMES IN THE MOURNING

Shards of my dreams scattered on the ground,
All my expectations crushed and dying,
Is there any hope left to be found?
My broken heart keeps crying.

Tears no longer satisfy the ache,
Sorrow too deep to express,
How much can I endure till I break?
When will I find blessed rest?

In the agonies of life, to whom shall I go?
I've no one, Lord, but you.
Even in this dire plight, I know
Earth's comfort never will do.

Surrounded by friends, yet alone in this pain,
I glimpse your precious trust.
From all of my loss, new perspective I gain.
You love me, though I am but dust!

My hurt, the window through which your love flows,
For though sorrow may last for the night.
Joy in the mourning you will bestow,
I find new hope in your light.

THE PAINFUL, BEAUTIFUL TRUTH

From the look on his face, I knew something was dreadfully wrong. But I was just a little indisposed for deep conversation, being firmly ensconced in the dentist chair for X-rays and a cleaning. He clutched Roman, our three-month-old, just a little too desperately, and his eyes seemed suddenly puffy. It dawned on me in that surreal instant that tragedy does not wait for a convenient moment to strike. When the hygienist left the room for a minute, Joel managed to say to me, "It's all my fault, and I'm going to jail."

"Just tell me what happened!" I demanded with a calm resolution my heart did not feel.

Haltingly, my beloved husband of nearly fifteen years confessed his secret obsession with pornography, an addiction that had spiraled downward to take the form of child pornography. He had just received a phone call from the church that was our landlord. They informed him that the police, who had been secretly tracking his internet activity, had arrived at our house that very morning with a search warrant and had confiscated all of our computers, hard drives, and other media. What timing—we were out of town on a ministry trip! The irony was painfully apparent, but I could not wrap my mind around it.

I do not remember much of what I said or what he said. Somehow we managed to finish our appointments. Both older boys needed an orthodontic consult for braces. But that did not even faze me. Suddenly the expense and inconvenience of braces seemed so commonplace. My whole life was falling apart. Who could think about braces? It was as if I could not even get my mind to work and to understand the normal, everyday things that were going on around me. I was in a total fog.

Joel and I had been missionaries with New Tribes Mission for over four years. We had spent three of those years serving as youth pastor and teacher at a mission school in Venezuela. Our lifelong dream was to serve God through ministering to missionary children (MK's). We were back in the United States in transition because the political situation in Venezuela had deteriorated so severely. As a result, the mission school where we worked had shrunk to less than half its original size and no longer needed our services. We had been living in the States for a year, working on partnership development and making plans to transition to another missionary school, possibly in the South Pacific.

Of course, I instinctively knew we would never work with MK's again. It was doubtful that we could be missionaries ever again or even plan on leaving the United States. Our whole life was changing; our future was spinning out of control.

Over the next several days I wandered around in a haze, walking and crying in the rain, poring over the psalms, clutching my infant son close for comfort and contemplating escape—one sharp turn of the wheel over a bridge or into oncoming traffic.

But I knew I couldn't. I had three precious boys who needed me. And I knew God would not let me be so reckless with the gift of life that He had given. But I did pray that maybe God would see fit to just let me die. He did not.

I remember praying desperately, "O God, you are good and do only good" (Psalms 119:49, paraphrased), as if it were the only string keeping me from utter desolation and complete insanity.

Jerry Sittser, in his book, A Grace Disguised, shares similar struggles. In one horrific car accident, his mother, wife, and young daughter were all killed. He suggests that "at the core of loss is the frightening truth of our own mortality." I was finding that to be profoundly true in my own life. My frailty was apparent in entirely new ways as I fought the gamut of raging emotions, from fear, to horror, to desperate sorrow.

One of the biggest struggles I faced was the randomness of pain and how tragedy strikes without warning. I was suddenly living in the middle of raw emotions all the time, while still having to listen to others discuss simple, everyday issues. People laughing and chatting about the most recent news in sports or the flavor of custard at Culvers just seemed so out of place to me. I wanted to scream, "Don't you know, none of that matters anymore? My world is falling apart. My beloved has betrayed me! Who cares about custard?" I knew I could not expect other people to enter into the pain I felt; it simply was not their pain to bear. It was mine. Further, most people I was interacting with did not even know I was facing such excruciating circumstances.

At first we really did not know how messy the situation would get. And we had no idea what had made the police suspicious of Joel's activities online. Joel talked on the phone with the police officer in charge of the case who told us it would be all right to continue our trip. We had planned to be gone for almost two more weeks. In some ways, this was a blessing, as we had a family wedding to attend, some time camping in the Black Hills on the agenda, and many friends and family to reconnect with. In other ways, every day seemed like a prolonging of the inevitable, and although I dreaded facing the music, part of me just wanted to get it over with.

The investigator in charge of the case had also told us that Joel would need to go in for a police interview when he got home, but it could take awhile for the investigation to be completed and for any potential arrest to occur. Thus the waiting game began.

Knowing so little, we decided not to tell everyone yet, though Joel did contact New Tribes Mission immediately, and he also spoke with one of the pastors at our home church.

I had no one to talk to. Since we were traveling, we were thousands of miles away from my sisters and parents. One of the most brutal struggles I faced in those early days was the overwhelming aloneness. Joel was really struggling with grief, guilt, frustration, and a sense of helplessness. He was also having to deal with related business—our position with New Tribes Mission, the pastors of our home church, and even acquiring a lawyer.

Joel did not think he deserved my love and forgiveness, although he knew I would never leave him. Looking back I realize he likely did not know how to meet me in my suffering without making the pain worse. It was as if he saw himself as salt and thought drawing close to me in my wounded state would only cause more excruciating pain. Both of us were experiencing such a torrent of raw emotions. I think Joel felt like he had no comfort to offer me. Parts of his clandestine life he just could not express in a way that I could comprehend.

So I found myself in a completely new situation, a path of agony and despair that I felt destined to walk alone, a hurt that my dearest friend and lover could not enter into with me. Yes, Joel was grieving. But we were not standing together against an outside force that had caused us immeasurable pain. Instead, Joel was recoiling at the horror of his own decisions and reaping the consequences his own sin had inflicted, while I was reeling from the utter impossibility of it all trying to process this blatant treachery on my beloved's part.

The Effects of the Potter/Clay Relationship

The first couple of nights after we were informed of the investigation, I could not sleep at all. I lay in bed trying to imagine what course my life would now take. And I prayed, begging God to free me from my torture and to comfort me in my agony. After all, my only hope was the intervention of a loving and powerful God. But God is not obligated to us in any way, and I was learning this firsthand.

I have often been frustrated with popular Christianity that asserts if we love and obey God, then God will bless us with good relationships, financial security, well-rounded children, a happy marriage, maybe a little extra money in the bank, and the list goes on and on. It is such a typical American way of thinking. What about the millions of Christians all around the world suffering daily with unsanitary living conditions? What about Chinese Christians and believers in other persecuted parts of the world, who suffer routinely for their faith? Many even go out as missionaries to their own people, often with only one pair of clothing to their name and no means to purchase more. Are they not serving God, often in a more dedicated way than many American Christians? The pieces of the blessing puzzle just do not fit together.

On the other hand, these Christians who lack material possessions, often have beautiful, vibrant testimonies. Stories arise from the persecuted church about God's miraculous hand of provision, His healing in lives, and His saving grace being experienced in the most unlikely places.

What this suggests is that the American Christian assessment of God's blessing and approval is faulty. Blessing, by definition, means something not merited. And I knew this.

I was not expecting God to come speedily to my aid because I was such an upright Christian with a long pedigree of service. But I was expecting that He would respond to my needs by filling my heart with His peace, because He is a loving God. I knew material blessings were not an indication of His care. But I was certain that experiencing spiritual peace and well-being was. Further, I was certain God would not want Joel in prison while I languished, raising three children alone. What I was begging Him for was a natural, good thing. God would come to my aid, if I just cried out to Him in honest humility.

However, no matter what our reasoning, God does not answer to us. We cannot pull out favorite Scriptures and wave them in God's face, demanding their fulfillment in our lives. And yet so often, that is exactly what we do. We become judge and jury, indicting and convicting God on the basis of His own Word and then demanding restitution. The arrogance of our expectations is stark and ugly when held in the light of His holiness, but we rarely see it in that light.

God is not surprised by our human tendency to make demands. In Isaiah 29:16, He says, "You turn things upside down, as if the potter were thought to be like the clay! Shall what is formed say to Him who formed it, 'He did not make me'? Can the pot say of the potter, 'He knows nothing'?" By nature the Creator/created relationship disallows us any right to make demands of God, and God makes that very clear.

Secondly, on the basis of His omniscience, we have no right to question Him or hold Him accountable to us. In Isaiah 55:8-10, God clearly distinguishes His wisdom from ours. "'For My thoughts are not your thoughts, neither are your ways my ways,' declares the Lord. 'As the heavens are higher than the earth, so are my ways higher than your ways and my thoughts than your thoughts.'"

One of the undeniable problems we face when using God's own promises to make demands of

Him is that our thoughts are not His thoughts. What He calls a blessing, we may call a misery. What He calls good, we might call onerous. What He calls beautiful, we might call painful. And get this: He is right! The Isaiah passage is clearly indicating that we are the ones who have it all wrong. It may seem upside down to call consequences a blessing, but that is certainly what God does. In Psalms 119:67 the author says, "Before I was afflicted, I went astray, but now I keep Your Word" (NKJV). He recognized that consequences had drawn him to God.

As I begged God for divine intervention, I felt a certain comfort in His love. At the same time, I also felt a distinct impatience growing within me. While I knew none of our pain was caused by God, I also knew that He cares for the innocent sufferer. That was me! That was my children! He was not the author of the sinful choices that had landed us on this path, but surely He could make things right in an instant and spare us the agony we were facing. Surely a good and loving God would want to resolve our problems in the least painful way possible. After all, if a friend came to me in dire need and I could meet her need in an immediate way that would solve the problem, I would do it without a second thought! So if God is a friend to the helpless and needy, then wouldn't He want to use all of His resources and power (which of course, are immeasurable) to come to the aid of a desperately needy friend?

Job's Example in Suffering

In the book of Job, we read the story of a man who was deeply afflicted by various trials that took from him nearly all he held dear. Often, tragedy comes upon us because of something we have done and some poor choice we have made. In Job's case, affliction did come upon him as a result of something he had done; it was not something sinful but rather something good. He walked in dedicated obedience to God. Having caught the eye of God as a faithful follower, he was offered to Satan as a pawn in a supernatural power struggle. God suggested that Job would remain faithful regardless of his circumstances. Satan, on the other hand, contended that should Job lose all the creature comforts he was so accustomed to, he would also lose hope in God and curse Him.

God allowed Satan to take everything Job had, even down to his health, so long as he did not take his life. Thus in one day, Job lost all his wealth and even his children. Shortly after that, he lost his own health and was plagued with painful boils all over his body.

After days of sitting in a sack cloth and ashes, which was the cultural way to mourn, he finally began to demand an explanation from God. In essence, he shook his fist at God and cried out, "You said You were good! Well if You really are, then why is all this happening to me? Haven't I always been faithful to You? I haven't done anything to deserve this. You are powerful! You could fix it! So why don't You?"

One might think that at this point God would feel appropriately rebuked for His handling of the "Job case." He would regret having dangled such a loyal servant in front of Satan as a prize to be fought over. And with kind and loving words, He would woo Job back to Him, promising attentiveness and help in

Job's moments of dire need. This is not the response we find at all! After all, Job was right on two counts at least: God is loving, and He is powerful. Job was actually right in his assessment of his service to God. He had always walked uprightly before God. But Job was wrong in expecting that these truths would automatically result in a scripted response from God.

God's response to Job was this: "Who is it that questions my wisdom with such ignorant words?…Where were you when I laid the earth's foundation? Tell me, if you know so much. Who laid off its dimensions and stretched out the surveying line? Who supports its foundations and who laid its cornerstone?…Have you ever commanded the morning to appear and caused the dawn to rise in the east?…Where does light come from and where does darkness go?" (Job 38:2-13, NLT portions). And that is just the beginning! For over seventy verses, God questioned Job, showing Job several key factors about the character and authority of God.

Foremost, He pointed out that Job answered to Him; He did not answer to Job. God's vast knowledge, control, and power are far beyond humanity's ability to even comprehend, much less contend with. God showed Job that as the great Creator and Sustainer of all things, He was ultimately responsible for the whole world.

This does not mean He does not care for each individual part of His creation. The second thing God pointed out to Job was that His care is also far beyond our ability to understand. And because of that, we cannot quantify His care in human terms.

We cannot demand the kind of care that we deem appropriate. What God does in the midst of our pain may seem self-serving, upside down, or unfair according to human wisdom. That is where trust comes in. We can know on the basis of God's Word that He is "...good and does only good" (Psalms 119:49, NLT).

Additionally, God showed Job his own frailties. God's vast wisdom and amazing power when pitted against the wisest of all human argument will show us to be frail, inept, needy, and without a case in the holy judgment hall of God.

At the end of the story, Job found himself standing before God, stripped of all earthly blessings, even his own health, and repenting in utter helplessness. He no longer demanded of God a change in his circumstances. Instead, He begged a just God to forgive him. I find his assertion, "Before I had only heard about you, now I have seen you face to face," (Job 42:5, NLT), at once confounding and yet somehow comforting.

Often as I have read the book of Job, I have struggled to understand God as He is portrayed in this story. How could a good God involve Himself in bargaining with Satan? How could He allow such devastation to apparently prove some cosmic point? How could He be silent and watch Job suffer such pain?

Since God is God, there was no real bargain. He is all-knowing. He did not have to prove anything to Satan. And He certainly was not looking to find out for Himself how faithful Job was.

Although at first glance it may seem that the suffering Job experienced was flippantly allowed (or worse, instigated) by an aloof, proud Authority attempting to show off, that is certainly not the case. Such an assessment completely contradicts all that God in His perfect character stands for. So what was God's intention in allowing Job to face such horrible loss?

Never, until my present affliction, have I thought that maybe, just maybe, God was giving Job a gift. And in the end, Job would find out it was a gift more precious than all the possessions, family, and health he had previously enjoyed.

As a matter of fact, I think that is exactly what Job was saying when he responded to God with, "Now I have seen you face to face." Job was asserting that through the unbelievable pain of suffering and the ultimate confrontation of the Almighty, he had come to a deeper relationship with a holy God. Before, his knowledge was untested, blind faith, as it were. After his trial, he had a deep and personal knowledge of God.

So what we are left with is this: God, in His awesome power and omniscience, knows exactly what each one of us needs to drive us into Him, and with loving hands, He gives us those gifts, sometimes through tears as He watches our agony, but always with a smile as He anticipates our downfall into His loving arms.

UPSIDE DOWN AND BACKWARD

The Ideal Match

Joel and I were both raised in Venezuela, South America, as the children of missionaries. Joel was born in Venezuela, just weeks before his parents moved to a remote, tribal village to plant a church. I was two when my parents moved to Venezuela. Although our families lived in distant parts of the country, we grew up together at the boarding school for missionaries' children. In fact, my parents were house parents at the school, and Joel was in our dorm for many years.

We were afforded every benefit of a godly heritage at school, in the dorm, and in our homes. We each accepted Christ as our personal Savior at a young age, under the guidance and teaching of our parents. We had daily Bible classes at school, corporate devotions in the dorm, and the positive influence of many Christian missionaries and teachers.

In addition to the biblical training we received, we lived in a beautiful, tropical location, surrounded by three diverse tribal groups. We were blessed to develop a multicultural view of the world and were challenged by the spiritual darkness that still pervades many corners of creation. In many ways, it was an idyllic childhood.

We had none of the modern conveniences that so many people in America take for granted. Our stove and fridge were gas because we only had electricity for a few hours every day. There was one large generator that provided electricity for the entire school base daily for specified hours. Even when the generator was running, we could not use all things electric, because it was not big enough to handle the load of certain electric devices. We did not mind living without electricity. It was a normal part of life to us. We did not miss television, because we had never had one. Video games were unheard of as well.

What we did have was a river to swim and play in, plenty of outdoor space to explore, and the familiarity of a close-knit community.

I remember first noticing Joel when I was about eight years old, and I had a crush on him on and off throughout our growing up years. In my sophomore year of high school, we began to "date," which in our world consisted of walking to and from school together, doing our homework together, and maybe taking walks or sitting outside together to watch the sunset.

The missionary boarding school had strict rules of conduct for dating individuals, and my parents also held a high standard for me personally. Even holding hands required a special occasion and specific permission from my father. This resulted in the forging of a close friendship and a deep bond over the course of our high-school dating life. Even though I was very young, by the time I was sixteen,

I was convinced that I would marry Joel. We were the perfect fit for each other.

My desire for God grew steadily during those years. And I remember being concerned that Joel too would hunger and thirst after God. We spent time together studying God's Word, and we both felt compelled to dedicate our lives to missionary service.

Our courting years were not perfect. I was devastated when Joel told me of the sexual abuse he had suffered from his paternal grandfather. He had never told anyone about it before, so sharing this with me was a huge step for him. My heart longed to comfort him and aid in the healing.

I, on the other hand, struggled with poor eating habits as a result of low self-esteem and dissatisfaction with my body. Joel was a kind and faithful force in turning my eyes away from myself and onto Christ. The difficulties we faced drew us closer, and we knew we were meant to spend the rest of our lives together.

As a dating couple, we spent nearly a year apart when Joel returned to the United States to attend Bible college in my senior year of high school. The pain of our separation tugged at my heart day after day. We had spent so much of our lives together that it just did not seem possible to live and breathe and continue in daily life without being side by side. I wrote long letters and waited eagerly for correspondence from him, but mail was slow in arriving. International mail took weeks, and then it could sit in town for up to a week before the mission plane made a flight out to the school base. We were both severely tried by our time of separation, and by the time I graduated and headed back to the United States myself, we were more convinced than ever that we were meant to spend the rest of our lives together.

My parents, however, were convinced that we were both still too young to make that kind of decision and commitment. They insisted we wait, at least until I had gone to Bible college as a single student for a while.

Finally, in the spring of the year following my graduation from high school, my parents gave Joel their blessing, and he surprised me with a ring for my nineteenth birthday! We were ecstatic as we began to plan the wedding and our new lives together. I was convinced, perhaps like every bride, that no one had ever been as happy as I was. We were soul mates, and we belonged together.

Joel and I had entered into the steps of a physical relationship very slowly over the four-year period of our dating, partially because of the rules at the mission school, and partially because of my parents' high standard for me. But our physical relationship was also guided by our own personal convictions about purity. Joel was my first kiss, and I was his. We wanted to honor God with our lives. And we also wanted to honor one another with the gift of purity on our wedding night. Consequently, throughout our engagement, we were very careful to avoid the natural temptations of a physical relationship. Joel and I both felt that if we could wait for each other before marriage, then that would be an indication of our fidelity within the marriage.

We had everything going for us. I remember shortly before our wedding my grandmother, who was my best friend, telling me, "Tabitha, don't you ever come complaining to me about Joel, saying you didn't know what you were getting into. If any young woman knows what she's getting in a man, it's you." I knew she was right. I did not expect any major surprises or bumps in our marriage. After all, we had known each other since childhood, dated for almost four years, had strong, supportive families to encourage us, and a deep commitment to serving the Lord. What more could we need?

Now here I was, fifteen years later, trudging up a hill on one of my long walks, trying to make sense of the mess we were in. It had only been a few days since the call had come in from the investigator. And in those few days, everything idyllic about my life had been turned upside down and backward. My perfect marriage had been robbed of its purity, robbed of its genuineness, and robbed of its simplicity. My husband, lover, and best friend was a traitor to everything we held dear.

I could not understand the deception; the betrayal was excruciating. How could Joel say he loved me and had never wanted anyone but me, and yet secretly have been viewing such graphic and offensive images? In the long months of the investigation, many people asked me if I struggled with anger toward Joel. I honestly answered that my heart was too broken to be angry. The hurt and disappointment were too deep to be expressed in anger, and although there were times when my initial response to a surface situation would be anger, deep in my heart, anger did not reside. The anguish of betrayal was too deep for anger.

Lessons on Betrayal from Joseph

The Bible is full of examples of people who went from a storybook existence to utter desolation. One that I am always blown away by is the account of Joseph and his brothers. Joseph was favored by his father and brought up with every possible advantage. Scripture tells us that because of this, his brothers hated him. As a result of that hatred, they betrayed him, selling him as a slave. He ended up far from his homeland, in Egypt.

To make matters worse, these brothers lied about their treachery to their father and left him grieving the death of his favored son! Their wickedness was exceptional. Their hearts had become calloused by resentment. But Joseph refused to become bitter by the betrayal of his own family.

Years later, the irony and redemption of this story unfolded when Joseph, who had become the high commander of the entire land of Egypt, provided food for his brothers. Without his kindness, they would have starved to death in the famine that ravaged the land. What an amazing flip! Joseph, the hated, betrayed, and rejected brother, became lord over his siblings and entire family. Talk about upside down and backward.

When Joseph had the chance to exact his revenge for their treatment of him, he refused. His words are stunning: "You intended to harm me, but God intended it all for good. He brought me to this position so I could save the lives of many people. No, don't be afraid. I will continue to take care of you and your children." What an amazing example of God's kindness and grace.

Clearly, Joseph chose forgiveness because his ultimate trust and hope were in God, not in man. Over a thousand years before God inspired Paul to pen "...all things work together for good to them that love Him (God) and are called according to His purpose" (Romans 8:28), Joseph lived out that truth in vibrant color, accepting each thing that happened to him as an opportunity for God to work good in his life. Because Joseph trusted God to take care of him, he could relinquish his own needs, seeking instead to glorify God with his actions and attitudes. Joseph's example is beautiful and compelling.

Lessons on Betrayal from Jesus

As I faced the anguish of betrayal, I found myself turning to the One who could understand the betrayal like no other. Judas's betrayal of Jesus must have been excruciating. But given the body of Scripture that speaks to the relationship that Jesus had with Peter, I think Peter's denial and escape were likely more excruciating for Jesus to bear. He had pored three years of His life into a deep, personal relationship with Peter. He'd healed Peter's mother-in-law, calmed the seas saving the fisherman's life, called Peter out of the boat to walk on water, and supervised the catch of the century.

Jesus had chosen Peter to be one of only three disciples who witnessed Him in all His heavenly glory on the Mount of Transfiguration. And Peter had been the one to proclaim, "You are the Christ, the Son of the living God" (Matt. 16:16, NKJV). He and Jesus had been together for many ups and downs over the three-year period of Jesus's public ministry; from the miraculous feeding of thousands of people to walking together on the stormy water of Galilee, they had done it all.

Jesus had warned Peter of his pending denial, but Peter had turned a deaf ear, insisting that he would be a faithful follower and friend. But instead, in one fear-drenched moment, Peter rejected Him, cursing up and down that he didn't even know Jesus. In Luke's gospel, these poignant words are recorded after the account of Peter's denial: "At that moment, the Lord turned and looked at Peter... And Peter left the courtyard, weeping bitterly" (Luke 22:61a, 62, NLT).

Peter could have stood up in that very moment and recanted his oath, admitting his friendship with Jesus, but he did not. The love he had for Jesus was overruled by the fear of what mortal men might do to him. Instead, he escaped into the night. But he escaped in great anguish, weeping bitterly.

I was feeling just a tiny bit of what Jesus must have felt when He turned His eyes on Peter, one of His closest friends, and saw the shame that Peter felt at denying Him. What agony to be facing His hour of greatest need in His earthly life and know that those dearest to Him would desert him. Jesus knows the pain of betrayal. He knows the indescribable grief I felt when I looked in Joel's face and saw the shame written there.

Peter likely saw himself as useless to the Savior after the way he had behaved on the night of Jesus's arrest. The guilt and shame were, I am sure, forefront in his mind when Jesus appeared to all the disciples together. How could Jesus ever forgive him? How could he forgive himself?

Jesus's kind and gentle grace in his approach to Peter is a beautiful example of the kind grace He uses to draw us back to Himself when we have succumbed to the temptation of sin in our own lives. The personal reconciliation of Christ and Peter is recorded in John's gospel. Jesus asked Peter three times, "Do you love me?" Peter answered with strong conviction that yes, he did. Each time, Jesus said to him, "Then take care of my sheep" (John 21:15-17, fragmented NLT). Jesus was essentially telling Peter, "You are still useful to Me, because you love Me. I am calling you to participate in My kingdom. Show Me you love Me by caring for My children." Jesus showed His forgiveness of Peter by affirming his value.

Jesus also assured Peter that through this and many other experiences in his journey with Christ, he would grow. He would change, becoming a faithful follower—faithful to the point of death. In essence, Jesus was saying to him, "You fled in fear when you saw what they were doing to Me. You were not willing to stand up and die for Me. But a day is coming when you will get a second chance, and you will not flee. You will offer up your life as a sweet sacrifice in faithful service to Me." Jesus offered Peter the kind of grace that was unconditional and yet fraught with expectation. It would reap a harvest of growth in Peter's life.

Joel too had shown me how remorseful he was for his own actions. And although he had not changed his behavior prior to being caught, he felt the anguish of the trap he had entangled himself in. A godly friend of mine wisely said of Joel, "I'm sure this is something he didn't want in his life either." But he had been ruled by his flesh, and not by his love for his Savior. Now that Joel's sin had been exposed, he expressed a desire to rid himself of such filth and live a life that exemplified his repentance and reliance on Christ.

Joel felt a strong connection with Peter in the months after his exposure. He journaled these parallels between his story and Peter's:

> Peter knew Christ! He had followed him for years, serving Him and loving Him passionately. He was with Jesus from the start of Jesus's ministry. He had seen supernatural healing and miracles. He was completely sold-out for Christ. He stepped out of the boat and in faith walked on water with Jesus. The wind caused him to falter, but he knew to Whom he could call for help: "Lord, save me!"
>
> He had great insight from God the Father as to who Jesus was and confidently made the proclamation, "You are the Christ, the Son of the living God." In Gethsemane he drew his sword to protect his Savior, with well-meaning foolishness. But later that same night, just as Christ had predicted, Peter denied Christ. When his entire world was falling down around him, when the way he thought things were supposed to go did not, he backed out and disowned his own Savior. But the Lord called to his attention his grievous sin through the crowing of the rooster, and Peter went out and wept bitterly.

I also knew Christ! I had followed Him for years, serving Him and loving Him passionately. I was a minister of Jesus. I had seen God do amazing things while growing up on the mission field. I was completely sold-out for Christ. I stepped out in faith and became a missionary, walking with Jesus. At times I did falter, but I always knew whom to call upon: "Lord, save me!" I, like Peter, knew that Jesus is the Christ, the Son of God. But much of my activity was well-meaning foolishness. Later when all my world was falling down around me and nothing was going the way I thought it should, I denied Christ with my actions. My very sin was a denial of His power in my life. I turned my back on my Savior, just as surely as Peter did, but not just for a moment like Peter, but for years and repeatedly.

As soon as the Lord brought my grievous sin to light, I also wept bitterly, knowing the pain I had caused Him and myself through my sin. Peter's heart and mine were broken when we came face-to-face with our betrayals. Peter learned his lesson and went on to preach boldly in the face of tremendous opposition. Ultimately he gave his life in service to his Savior. God used him mightily in His kingdom. I can only hope that having followed in Peter's betrayal, I might also follow in his footsteps to become a vessel God can use to accomplish His purposes.

I found great comfort and insight in Christ's example, knowing His strength in me would give me courage to endure the agony of betrayal and loss. Christ was not interested in seeing Peter pay for his denial. Nor was He intent on making a public example of Peter. Jesus looked into Peter's heart and saw his genuine repentance. Jesus longed for Peter to experience a restored relationship with Him, and that is what He offered. In spite of the personal pain inflicted on Him, Jesus looked at the situation from the perspective of drawing Peter back to Him. He took the initiative of restoration. Christ would work this kind of forgiveness in my heart toward Joel. And I knew Joel would find that forgiveness from Christ too, that same call to follow Him, and the same assurance of his value as he sought Christ.

From our idyllic childhood and storybook courtship to the broken mess we found ourselves in, everything in our world had been turned upside down. But one thing remained the same. Hebrews 13:8 proclaims, "Jesus Christ is the same yesterday, today, and forever" (NLT). When my whole life was flying out of control, I found the bedrock of His faithful love firm beneath my flailing feet.

THE BATTLE OF PRIDE

Here I am Lord, Send me

Joel and I had gone to Venezuela in 2004 after years of college, training, and partnership development, with high hopes of settling there for a long career as missionaries. Our first year there, we entrenched ourselves in the ministry. Joel was learning the language at the same time that he was teaching at the school, assisting with airport runs for traveling missionaries and spearheading a youth program for the missionary children. I jumped right into teaching at the school and enrolled our youngest son, then two, in a local Venezuelan preschool. Our oldest went to school with me. Our schedule was busy but fulfilling.

My parents lived less than a mile away and were a tremendous help in our acclimation to the area. Joel's parents were also still ministering in Venezuela but lived in a tribal village about eight hours from the town where we worked. They made occasional trips to town for various reasons though, so we saw them periodically as well and always enjoyed hosting them in our home.

Our second year on the field, we got a dog for the kids and bought a house a little ways out of town with a big-enough living room to have youth events. Although certain areas of the Venezuelan culture still mystified us, we were beginning to feel at home. Our children were beginning to play with the neighbor kids, and we had made a few national friends. But our long-term plans of ministering in Venezuela were about to come to a grinding halt. In October of our second year, the president of the country announced his intention to expel missionaries from all tribal areas.

The next several months were stressful for us as we watched so many of our fellow workers leave their ministries in tribal locations and return to the States. Our youth group dwindled from twenty kids to seven in one year. Many of the students whose lives we had invested in were suddenly gone. Our coworkers with whom we had shared so much over the time we had been there also began to move out.

The political situation in the country was unstable, and the unrest around us was unsettling. We talked of escape plans if civil war broke out. Americans were hated by many, so we tried to maintain a low profile.

Our ministry was drying up before our eyes. Our dreams of living near family and working at the mission school were disintegrating. My heart cried out to God, "Why did you send us here just to have us leave in a few years? Why all the work? Why all the stress of moving and adjusting to a new culture?" I remember vividly one evening as I lay in bed, sobbing as if my very life were being drawn out of me. I cried for all the dreams that were dying. I cried for all the pain of uprooting our family that I saw in our future. I cried because I knew my life would never be the same.

Although Joel and I both suffered much of the stress of this time together, I did not really know or understand the toll it was taking on Joel. And he was pretty good at covering up the tension. Anger was building on the inside, but he maintained a calm façade as we accepted the inevitable and began to pack up for a move back to the United States.

Joel felt the burden of responsibility for our family very keenly in the face of potential physical danger. He also struggled with questions about our future, such as how to provide for the family and whether to continue in ministry on another field. If so, where and how soon?

This is what he shared about that struggle in a letter to a close friend, written nearly a year after his incarceration.

> I was mad at God for how things in my real life were turning out. If God was in control of real life and He had made such a mess of things for me, then guess what! My fantasy life was going to be my own to rule any way I wanted. The more it flew in the face of His Holiness, the better. So why not!

> I don't know when exactly it started that year. But I began to spend more and more time downloading and watching inappropriate material from the Net. I gave in to an addiction to pornography that I had battled for years.

Joel internalized these emotions, the anger toward God, and the justification of his sin. He did not share those feelings with me until years later, admitting too that he had believed Satan's lie that he could separate his cyber life from real life.

We arrived back in the United States in May of 2007, nearly three years after our departure, exhausted emotionally, physically, and mentally. I will never forget the elation I felt as we stood in Customs and Immigration in Miami, knowing that we were safe and back in our own homeland. But with that elation came a great sense of emptiness. We did not really belong anywhere.

Unfortunately, neither of us was brave enough or humble enough to seek help for our weary, battered hearts as we returned. After all, we were the missionaries. It was one thing to be tired and sad. It was quite another to be an emotional, directionless wreck. So instead of processing our emotions and dealing with the grief of our displacement from Venezuela, we gathered the tattered edges of our ministry garments and wrapped them around our spiritual pride as gamely as we could.

Within a few weeks of being back in the United States, we began working with the youth group in our church and researching options for assignment to another overseas mission school. Little did I know then that God was about to stop us in our tracks and force us to take stock of our lives in a whole new way.

Pride Exposed

In the very first days of knowing the horrible truth, I remember asking, "Why me? What in the world happened to land me in this mess?" I even looked at other Christian couples and wondered what made them so much better than me. Why did I deserve to suffer like I was? Why weren't other couples with a less-than-perfect pedigree suffering? What was different between them and me? I wanted so badly to find some reason and to make some sense of the agonies I faced. And I longed to know that it was not my fault. If I had to suffer unjustly, I wanted to be sure that the injustice was recognized and possibly fixed.

On the other hand, deep down inside, a part of me wondered if some of this was my fault. Had I overlooked some need in Joel's life? Had I been less than attentive to him? Was I flawed? I began to wonder if the happiness I perceived in our relationship was a farce. Perhaps Joel had never been happy with me. Maybe he was disillusioned with our life because I was a colossal disappointment to him as a wife and partner.

Joel and I have always been kindred spirits. We were best friends before we started dating and had years of experience with honesty and faithfulness. We both really loved God and longed to serve Him overseas.

Early in our marriage, Joel had admitted a struggle with pornography which he at first justified as natural male behavior. We grappled with the issue on and off for several years. Joel would try to stop and be consistent for a while. But it always seemed like there would be another slip. These always made me feel like Joel did not really care that much. He was not convinced of the asinine nature of this problem. But at the same time, I also felt like making too much of the slips would only discourage Joel. I wanted him to know that I was with him in this and would help him grow out of the temptation. In return, I guess I expected honesty from Joel in the way he handled this struggle. I did not make a huge deal out of it or issue demands, so I hoped he would respond by letting me into the private world of this struggle.

Finally in 2001, with the help of an accountability friend and other changes in our lives, Joel seemed to totally close the door on that issue. At last, I saw a real change in his attitude toward pornography. He no longer justified it, but viewed it as a sinful habit. We had faced this struggle together. I felt that my honest grace toward Joel would compel him to be forthright with me in the future about this struggle if it ever arose again, which I was confident it would not.

Even though I did not expect it, I felt like I knew Joel well enough to tell if the issue of pornography was to again take hold in his life. I wondered how women could be fooled by unfaithful husbands. I just imagined that they did not have the wonderful marriage relationship I enjoyed with Joel.

Of course, although I did not realize it, I was totally ignorant of the nature of addictions. And without meaning to, I had laid expectations on Joel by the very grace I patted myself on the back for extending to him. Nate Larkin in his book, *Samson and the Pirate Monks,* tells the candid story of his downward spiral into the world of sex addiction. At one point he makes this comment regarding his addictive behaviors: "A nightmare was hurtling in my direction and there was nothing I could do to stop it; it was going to hit me and it was going to hurt."[i]

Joel too has expressed to me how irrational his thinking became the more entrenched he was in pornography. He expressed it this way: "I wasn't in my right mind during those times." It was not till much later in our journey that I began to understand some of the issues related to addictive behaviors and how those had affected Joel. At the time, I was operating on a totally different plane.

Once I became aware of the ugly truth, I wondered how long I had been duped. I felt like such a fool. How could I have thought we were so happy while he was seeking satisfaction in cyberspace? How could someone who loved me, and knew I loved him, have been so deceptive with me? And again, the nagging question: Was I somehow to blame?

Joel made every effort from the very beginning to assure me that I was in no way responsible. He insisted that it was his problem—his fault. Often, he reiterated that his secrecy had nothing to do with me; it was not a matter of how much I loved him or he loved me. It was hard—nearly impossible in the state I was in—to believe him, although much later in our journey, I have come to understand that he was telling me the truth. Again this is a common thread with addictive behaviors, one I was ill-equipped to deal with.

Alone in my agony, with crazy questions bouncing around in my head, the only comfort I found in those first days was in God's Word and my conversations with God during long walks, often in the rain.

Random Pain and Senseless Questions

I knew there was no sense in what I was doing, but I found myself comparing the plight I was in with the circumstances of others around me. I didn't want to win the "Most Painful Tragedy Award." As a matter of fact, I didn't even want to be a contender for that award. But somehow at times, I found strange relief in the awareness that I was not the only one suffering deeply. On the other hand, I also found myself battling with anger and righteous indignation as I watched other people who were in my mind less deserving than I, living relatively pain-free lives. Even more perplexing for me was the anger that arose when someone implied that my suffering was not as great as theirs. Why do we feel some desperate need to be recognized for our pain?

Wrestling with grief over his horrific loss, Sittser wrote: "...I question whether experiences of such severe loss can be quantified or compared. Loss is loss, whatever the circumstances. All losses are bad, only bad in different ways. No two losses are ever the same. Each loss stands on its own and inflicts a unique kind of pain. What makes each loss so catastrophic is its devastating, cumulative, and irreversible nature."[ii]

Carol Kent, well-known author and speaker, shares a beautiful testimony about her family's incredible loss. Their only son is incarcerated for murder with a lifetime sentence, yet she speaks boldly of God's faithfulness to them in the midst of the agony. She also discusses how people have a tendency to quantify and qualify pain. She, like Sittser, insists that every pain, though different, cannot be qualified as more or less intense. She has repeated over and over, "Pain is pain is pain."[iii]

I too began to realize that the intense loss I felt could not be justified. There was no comparison chart that could possibly make me feel better. No neat box of textbook explanations or expected outcomes could be built around my current situation that would make me feel the sudden relief of reason. My grief was deep and intense, and it swallowed up reason.

Even though I did not really feel like I was receiving any grand revelation from God, He was at work in my heart. In the very first, painful days, He was showing me my own pride in the reactions I was having to people around me.

Why did I imagine myself to be less deserving of pain and suffering than the people around me? Could it be that I loved myself more than them? And what makes us deserving of pain, anyways? It is pure human reason that causes us to weigh and measure pain and estimate how much each person deserves. Did I deserve the pain I was in more than the people around me? Did they deserve to suffer too? People seemingly suffer randomly, whether they are esteemed as deserving of it or not. My challenge was relinquishing those natural, human ideals that cried out to me: only those who really deserve it should suffer, not you!

Carrying On

Four days after we received the phone call informing us of the investigation into Joel's Internet behavior, we met with Joel's parents to travel west from Wisconsin to South Dakota for a family vacation. We had planned to spend four days in the Black Hills camping and then drive to Nebraska for a family wedding.

Months earlier we had planned this trip. With great anticipation, I had researched popular tourist sites and campgrounds. The boys and I had been counting how many new states we'd hit on the drive. Joel's parents had a pop-up camper which made the prospect of camping sound cozy, even though in late spring at a mile-high elevation, the weather promised to be nippy.

Since we were missionaries, most of our travel was with the purpose of sharing in churches, seeing friends, and visiting family. Camping in the Black Hills was a real splurge for our family. Now, even though I still didn't want to miss it, I was not sure I could endure it either. I was caught in the strange vortex of needing to carry on with normal activity and wanting nothing more than to collapse and never face life again.

We had not told the kids that anything was amiss. Marshall was about to turn ten and Jaden was only six. Roman, our youngest, was only three months old. There was no way they could understand what all this was about. And this vacation was for them, too. I knew we had to pull it together and enjoy our time as a family, even though in the back of my mind I kept thinking, This might be the last vacation we get to take all together. And while that thought came with a sense of desperation, it carried with it a mandate that we make the most of this time.

So I found myself attempting to make sense of the mess in my mind and live a relatively normal life on the surface. While my thoughts were running in a hundred different directions, I was trying to force myself to think about what kind of food would be the easiest to serve from a camper or to cook over a fire.

Joel had not talked to his parents yet about the investigation, so on our first day of travel, he rode with them and told them the story. Even though I was not with them, my heart was in agony the entire time as I drove our van with the three boys. Strangely I also felt a huge sense of relief that someone else was going to know what was going on with us, and I was no longer going to have to pretend that everything was normal all the time. I would have someone to talk to about all the questions and unknowns we were facing. We have always been very close to Joel's parents, and it did help immensely to be able to talk to them about the situation. It was a comfort to my heart just knowing that they were in this with me. I knew they would do anything they could to help us get through it.

But I also faced seeing their pain and their unanswered questions firsthand. Like me, Joel's dad began to blame himself, wondering if there was something he could have done differently in rearing Joel. His mom was obviously deeply hurt and even angry at Joel for his sinful choices. And as his mother, she was not afraid to ask some painful and stinging questions. However, both of his parents chose forgiveness and loving support.

The first night of our trip, I got a call from one of my friends back in Florida who had heard what had happened. I remember trying so hard not to cry on the phone as I said to her, "For the rest of my life, people are going to look at me one of two ways: pity or scorn, and I don't want either!" I was desperately afraid of what people would think of us. And I did not think I could stand being pitied any more than I could handle people's scorn.

Again, I was battling with preconceived ideas and standards that we as a family no longer measured up to. I was devastated by the thought of other Christians shaking their heads and murmuring under their breath about my husband, about me, about our family! We would become another statistic in someone's catalogue of how those in ministry cave to the pressures of secret sins. We would be a part of the attrition rate for our mission board! I hated the thought of it.

All of this culminated into a tornado of frenzied thoughts filling my mind. The pride I felt in comparing myself to others did not dissipate when I examined my life for its own merit. I had been faithful and obedient in the life God had given me. In me welled up a certain expectation of recompense. I deserved so much better!

Not only had I been faithful and obedient, but I had carefully guarded my life from pitfalls worthy of judgment or punishment. Even though I knew it was skewed theology, I could not help but wonder what I had done to deserve this. Why was I suddenly facing scorn, ridicule, and possibly the kind of pity offered out of condescension? I knew as I faced these questions that strongholds in my heart were being torn down by a loving but determined and sovereign God.

Learning to be Needy

I have always been an outspoken, friendly, independent person. I love to learn. I am excited to try new things, and I never shy away from an opportunity to share my opinion. Along with that, I was reared in a Christian home and was afforded the benefit of intense Bible training throughout my childhood. I attended Bible college and received my bachelor's degree in Christian education. Studying God's Word has long been a personal habit, and I deeply desire to grow in a relationship with my Savior.

Furthermore, I am a natural problem solver. I am the kind of person who loves a challenge. I see the drop in the bottom of the bucket and say, "Thank heaven it isn't empty!" Lemons can be easily made into lemonade, and why not?

This positive outlook was tested in a new way when I faced my husband's betrayal and possible incarceration. I certainly did not know how to make lemonade out of these lemons. But neither did I know how to be needy. I did not know how to survive without attempting to fix it.

My friendships were based on equal give and take, but most of the time, if there was an upset, it was in the direction of giving. My life was easy; my marriage was solid. I had something to give. And I was happy to do it. I did not know that a subtle pride had moved into my heart, insulating me from ever being the vulnerable friend in a relationship.

Early in our journey, I was desperate for a good friend with whom I could be needy, yet I didn't know how to be needy. I was beginning to see how much humility it takes to express neediness. The core issue was that I feared rejection. Who wanted to deal with high-maintenance situations? My struggle was exacerbated by our recent move to Florida from the mission field. Many of my closest friends were living thousands of miles away.

God was at work in this void as well, peeling away my layers of pride. At Joel's prompting, I asked a casual friend from the school our kids attended to go to lunch with me one day. What resulted was a heartfelt, brutally honest conversation that has led to one of my closest friendships. Perhaps that is because this wonderful woman of God was not afraid to hit me over the head with the two by four of my own pride. At one point in our conversation, I was expressing to her my discomfort in being needy. She looked me straight in the eye and said, "Hmm…a little issue with pride going on there, Tabitha?"

Of course, that is exactly what held me captive.

The Pride of the Righteous

In the story of Job, three friends showed up and mourned with him, sitting silently for seven days in sack cloths and ashes. If these friends had gotten up and left after those seven days, they would have done well. Instead, for human reasons alone, they decided to stay and minister to Job, giving him some spiritual explanations for all he was suffering. Their primary contention was that Job deserved the suffering he was experiencing, and if he would only admit and confess his sin, things would become better.

Their argument is solidly based on the erroneous assumption that we can control our world by how we behave. If we do good things, then our lives will go smoothly. If we do bad things, life will be miserable. On top of this gigantic chunk of deception was the icing of their own blatant pride. So many times, we can offer someone assistance out of pride. We can make spiritual suggestions and observations from a pedestal high above them. This is exactly what Job's friends did. Their implication was, "We aren't suffering like you, because we have not sinned like you."

Job had responded admirably to the indescribable pain he was suffering before these three friends showed up. He had rightly acknowledged God's sovereignty, saying, "The Lord gave me what I had, and the Lord has taken it away. Praise the name of the Lord" (Job 1:21, NLT). He had even told his wife that she was speaking only foolishness when she suggested he curse God and die rather than continue suffering. He asked her, "Should we accept good things from the Lord, and never anything bad?" (Job 2:10, NLT). Scripture tells us that up to that point, Job did not sin by blaming God.

However, once his friends badgered Job with their arguments and assumptions about his guilt, he began to feel pretty undeserving of his trial. He was ready to speak out in his own defense. Never mind defending the Lord and His sovereignty. Job had done that, and still he was suffering. He cried out to God, "Why do you torment me?" Job expressed openly and heatedly that he felt God was being unjust by allowing him to suffer.

Unlike his friends, Job knew that God was the giver of both bad and good, and one's behavior does not necessarily secure one result or the other. But Job still felt justified in demanding an answer from God. This justification comes from a heart of pride, a heart that believes that if nothing else, at the very least, it deserves answers.

So often in our damaged efforts to reconcile God's goodness and our present painful circumstances, we claim promises of God as our due. We assume He is obligated to respond in a certain way to our needs in order to comply with His own established standard—indeed in accordance with His own character. The things we trust Him for are good things. Since He is a good God who "from His hand satisfies the desire of every living thing" (Psalms 145:16, NLT), then surely He will meet our need with the good thing we desire.

Much is assumed in this self-reliant, bulletproof form of trust. Not the least of those assumptions is that God defines "good" in the same manner that we do. We also assume that God will enter into our bargaining and hold up His end as long as we fulfill ours. The final and possibly most damaging assumption we make is that our response is a spiritual one. Self-righteousness wears a white robe. Pride calls the shots, and we are disillusioned when God doesn't respond according to our expectations.

Do the Innocent Suffer?

I studied for two years at a secular college before transferring to a Christian college. One of my classes was medieval humanities, which covered much of the period we call the "Early Church" era. In a completely secular setting, we discussed the book of Job as a work of literature attempting to solve the problem of a good, sovereign God, and a world full of innocent people who suffer. This was a fascinating class for me, as I listened to unregenerate minds grappling with and attempting to understand the existence of both God and suffering. Many nonbelievers give up on solving this dilemma in disgust, claiming that since the two can't possibly coexist, then one must not. Clearly suffering exists. Therefore a good, sovereign God must not. What a sad and misguided conclusion.

Actually, the question, "Why do the innocent suffer?" is an unfounded one. According to God's Word, all people are born sinners and are therefore enemies of God. While it is certainly true that some people suffer innocently in the sense that they committed no offense that resulted in their suffering, no one is actually innocent.

Every person has sinned and is therefore responsible before a holy God. One of my favorite speakers, Pete Briscoe, made the comment once that while we all know "two wrongs don't make a right," it is also true that two rights cannot right a wrong. No matter how much right we ever do, we cannot right our wrongs. When we question our suffering on the basis of innocence, it is because of a defective worldview and a lack of understanding of sin.

Another problem with the question of why the innocent suffer is the idea that what we do (or do not do) is the sole factor in whether we experience good things or bad. The question comes from a one-dimensional view of life while God, the Creator, Sustainer, and Sovereign over all things, has created life to be multidimensional. Innumerable factors contribute to the experiences we have in life.

To boil down those experiences as solely contingent on our behavior is totally simplistic.

Equality and Justice for All

I find that my sense of justice demands equitable consequences for offenses. People make poor choices every day that result in devastating consequences. A simple example would be driving too fast. It is a poor choice, but does the person who is careless and drives too fast deserve the consequence of being in a car accident and killing someone he loves? What about the child who refuses to obey quickly and walks out onto the street rather than turning around when his mother calls to him? It is disobedience, but is it deserving of death? If that child were struck by a car, would anyone say, "Well he got what he deserved for disobeying"? Of course not!

Choices in this world inevitably lead to consequences, but we can't demand that those consequences fit the crime. As Americans, we feel that it is an inalienable right that we not suffer "cruel and unusual punishment." While our justice system must adhere to that mandate, real-life situations often result in cruel and unusual outcomes that cannot be controlled. The truth is that life and consequences don't always make sense.

Sin has warped every aspect of our world. As a result, suffering will occur, in small or great measure, sometimes as the result of poor choices and sometimes with no visible cause at all. Pride in me wanted to demand better and wanted to insist that I was undeserving of the suffering I now experienced.

But the truth kept shouting, "It doesn't matter who you are; suffering is a part of life in a fallen world, where no one is completely innocent." I did not like this answer, so I just kept clinging to my pride and feeling justified in my sense of injustice at all that I was made to suffer. It did not make anything better.

The Classroom of Suffering

As much as we strive to avoid pain, there is no classroom like that of suffering to throw us upon the mercies of God. Our desire for God when life is successful consists often as a desire to use Him, not know Him or enjoy Him. When we are satisfied from other cisterns, our souls are not parched for the refreshing water of God's mercy. And, when in the midst of our pain, we demand mercy, our capacity to receive it is barricaded by pride. Our neediness is a platform for Him to showcase His mercy only when humility and desperation throw open the curtain to center stage; and even then, it may not play out in the way that we anticipate.

When I was a little girl of six, my family lived in a remote tribal location in Venezuela. My sister, Tammy, and I are only eighteen months apart in age and were best friends and worst enemies all at the same time. We had no other children of our own culture to play with though, so we spent many hours together.

Our house and one other block house, as well as a few small outbuildings, sat next to a grass airstrip used by the mission plane to bring us supplies. The Indians' tribal roundhouse was at the other end of the airstrip. Just a short walk down a jungle trail was the river. We had a fenced-in backyard where we were allowed to play without supervision. At the back of the yard was a hot pepper plant that produced the hottest red peppers you could imagine. The juice is so potent that it burns the hands. The tribal people loved these peppers for seasoning their food. But they also used the juice as a form of punishment for children who were defiant.

My parents had carefully warned my sister Tammy and me to stay away from those peppers. They had reiterated that we were not even to pick them because the juice might burn us. My sister was older and wiser than I, but I was the one that created all the fun (and trouble). She was inclined to obey anything my parents said, just because it was easier than risking a negative consequence. While I wanted to be good, I really did, I just couldn't imagine obeying everything to the letter all the time. Surely there was some wiggle room on some of the regulations.

One day, I suggested that we just try one pepper. To convince Tammy to participate, I said we could just share one. We did not each have to eat our own. And surely one tiny pepper shared between the two of us couldn't cause that much pain.

Talk about learning firsthand! The pain was intense and searing. We ran screaming to the house, our mouths and hands on fire. I don't remember any form of discipline being meted out for our disobedience. I think my parents knew that we had learned our lesson from the intense pain of our poor choice.

I learned a lot more than just to avoid those peppers. I learned that my parents were telling the truth and that I could save myself much trouble by believing them. The classroom of pain led me to trust them and know they had my best interest at heart. I would like to say that Tammy learned her lesson and quit being influenced by my crazy schemes, but we were kids and still had plenty of growing up to do.

But I Don't Want to Go to School!

No one wants to suffer. It would be masochistic to seek out pain, even in the interest of personal growth. Most of us hope we can learn what we need to with minimal pain. The classroom of suffering is naturally avoided at all cost. The problem is that as humans, we can't avoid it forever. Recently I read that the one common thread running through all humanity is suffering. Of course, suffering comes in different measures.

I remember early in this trial finding it offensive when someone suggested that suffering is the only true schoolmaster that draws us into a deeper relationship with God. Wouldn't that make God a sadist who is desirous of our suffering to make of us what He wants? And we know that is impossible. God doesn't enjoy putting us through pain! However, God in His sovereignty knows that pain is not the worst thing that could happen to us. A life without knowing Him is. Our lives are but a vapor. No matter how intense the pain we feel, it will not last forever. In the middle of pain, that is really very little comfort. What is a greater comfort is knowing that God is in the pain with us.

I imagined the shame our family would face, and it was crushing. My fear that people would label me or my family was evidence of the pride that sought to control me. I wanted to prove to my friends, my family, and other Christians that I was a strong person and that I could deal with this suffering in a dignified manner. As I told one friend on the phone just days into this trial, "I don't want people to think I'm stuck with Joel, because I'm not."

I could just imagine people shaking their heads sadly and commenting on what a pickle I was in, stuck in a marriage with a criminal pervert. I did not want them to look on my husband, whom I still loved very much, with that kind of scorn, and I certainly did not want them to think I was stuck! I was not staying with Joel because I was pitiful and weak; I was staying with him because I loved him, and I knew God wanted me to stay with him! Pride, disguised as human dignity, had wrapped itself around my heart like a protective bandage, and it was going to take the Eternal Surgeon's hands to successfully remove it.

It was hard to focus on truth when I was blinded by my own perceptions. It was hard to focus on truth when the truth was painful. And the truth was I knew that Joel and I were both going to face much ridicule, scorn, and pity. I knew we were going to suffer the loss of our ministry to youth, our full-time jobs as missionaries with New Tribes Mission, and perhaps most painfully, our reputation.

I knew that Joel's shame in many ways would also be mine. And what I was surprised to find was that I loved him enough to want to bear that shame with him. No, I hadn't committed the crime. I hadn't been involved in a graphic, clandestine, and socially disgusting sin, but I was willing to stand beside my husband who had, because I loved him.

This gave me a tiny glimpse into the kind of love Jesus has for us. I saw Him willingly standing with us as we faced the shame of sinful choices. And I remembered that He bore the shame of being "counted among the rebels" (Isaiah 53:12, NLT) for our sake. He began to show me that the real shame was not that my reputation would be sullied but that His would be. This was the beginning of the Surgeon's hand at work in my heart, carving away my pride and building a humility and compassion that can only come from a supernatural source.

THE AGONY OF WAITING

Fear of the Unknown

What I did not know at the beginning of this trial was how long the process of investigating Joel's criminal behavior would take. Though I dreaded the outcome, I also longed for it, because the waiting was so painful and uncertain.

Upon completing our vacation and returning to Florida, Joel had to go in to the local police station and give his statement. I remember that last day of driving back toward Florida as a major low point. Although the entire vacation had been shadowed by the upcoming drama about to unfold upon our return, it had been time spent together outside of the horrendous trial we were about to face. Now, the shadow was becoming a reality looming over us as the miles ticked away toward home.

I did not know if our house would look totally ransacked like in the movies when the police search a place, or if anything would even seem amiss when we arrived. I dreaded pulling into the driveway and finding out. There was no one to meet us and go through this with us. We arrived home late at night, and Joel cautiously entered the house. Much to our relief, most of it looked exactly as we had left it, except for the gaping emptiness and wires on the floor where Joel's computer had been.

We found out later that a couple of the guys whom Joel had discipled in the youth group of our church had come over to the house and cleaned everything up for us. Although they were never completely clear on what all the police had been through, they did say that it was a mess, with drawers of things dumped out everywhere. God knew exactly how much we could take coming back home to this situation, and I cannot thank Him enough for putting it on their hearts to come in and clean up for us. It spoke volumes to us of God's love and forgiveness. These young men will probably never realize what ministers they were to us in their simple act of service.

Our first several days back in Florida were a whirlwind of meetings with church leaders, mission leaders, the investigating officers, family, and friends. Some of those meetings were reassuring; some were pure torture; and all were emotionally draining. Joel did his best to carry the burden of these difficult meetings, and he went to many of them without me.

One of the most difficult parts of this process was the response of our home church. Having met with Joel and me, the elder board asked that Joel not attend church or have any contact with the youth, former youth, or their families. They also wrote a letter explaining the investigation into Joel's conduct and sent it to every family whose kids were in the youth group. We had been members of the church for over fourteen years and had served in many different capacities. This was our Stateside Christian community. Being cut off from our church body and friends like this at a time when we needed them so badly was hurtful beyond words. It left us feeling isolated, as if we were quarantined with a deadly disease.

Our church called these steps "church discipline." But this was confusing to us because Joel was already deeply penitent, and the purpose of biblical church discipline is to induce repentance in the wayward individual. However, it was hard for some to accept Joel's repentance without seeing quantifiable evidence of it. One member of the church suggested that Joel was only repentant because he had been caught. As much as we understood that kind of sentiment, it was still hurtful.

Joel and I both gained comfort from the story of David's repentance in the face of the Prophet Nathan's accusations. David was the king of Israel. He was wealthy, prestigious, and famous. He had everything he could need, and God had been tremendously close to David. Yet when David lusted after another man's wife, he chose the sins of adultery and murder rather than reliance on God and thankfulness. His deception remained unknown for over a year. Whether David felt any remorse during that period of time is not recorded in Scripture. The indication is that he did not expect consequences. He thought he'd covered his tracks pretty well. But God knew. He sent Nathan to David with a parable to show David the depth of his sinful choices and their resulting consequences. David's response was immediate confession. He told Nathan that he had indeed sinned grievously against God and was tremendously sorrowful. When his sin was exposed, David saw it as a horrific affront to a holy God, and this brought him to a point of total repentance. Joel related to this response and was comforted to know that God did not find his repentance to be simply a sorry-to-be-caught kind of repentance.

We also had to resign from New Tribes Mission, our livelihood and lifelong dream. Our future plans and present ministry were, understandably, stripped away.

Since we were living in the church's mission home, this also meant we had to move. By God's kind hand of direction, we had already been planning to move within the next six months, and before our trip up north, we had put an offer in on a small house. The offer had been accepted, so at least we had somewhere to go. But moving in my current state of mind, while continuing to maintain a sense of reasonable normalcy for the kids, seemed impossible. And we weren't going to receive any physical help from people in the church, since we'd been instructed to avoid any contact with them.

Intense Interview

On the Friday after we returned home, Joel went to the police station alone to meet with the investigator of the case. I was petrified as he left, hugging him and kissing him with marked desperation. Although we'd been assured that this was a routine interview, I feared they would arrest Joel on the spot, being totally ignorant of law-enforcement protocol.

My sister came to spend the day with me and help me pack. I had to do something so I wouldn't go crazy with worry. We prayed together and worked together for most of the morning, and my heart skipped a beat when Joel called around noon to say he was on his way home. He sounded good, and I couldn't wait to talk to him more when he arrived home.

His explanation of the meeting was lengthy, but what stuck out to me was his story of taking a voice-stress analysis test, the newest type of lie-detector test. He had voluntarily submitted to one without the advice of an attorney, which surprised me. When I commented on that, he said, "I did it mostly for you. I wanted you to know it is true when I say I've never touched anyone, underage or not, inappropriately." Although I was relieved by the results of this test, I had not really expected otherwise. Perhaps I just could not imagine that things could get worse. But I think it was because I knew Joel was not a pedophile. Joel went on to say that he had been scared to take the test, fearful that nerves would skew the results, but in the end he had passed with no red flags or areas of concern whatsoever and was relieved to have that evidence in his corner.

We both knew that once people heard what Joel was under investigation for, they would assume he was a pedophile and would begin to look for victims. It was part of the burden we would both deal with. It was part of the shame we now lived with.

But I was honestly relieved to know he was not only telling me the truth but was willing to subject himself to being tested by the police force to prove it. It was one small evidence to me of his love for me and longing to make things right. It also showed me that he was willing to accept that his word was no longer enough. He understood that his own credibility had been stripped away, and he didn't expect me to forgive and forget.

The officer Joel had interviewed with told him that typically this kind of case takes around three months to investigate before an arrest or further action occurs. She also said that based on Joel's cooperation up to that point, if an arrest were necessary, Joel would be notified and required to turn himself in. This, of course, made us feel a little more at ease. I no longer held my breath each time a police siren resounded in the distance, sure they were headed right for our house.

We had lost our livelihood and our ministry and were in the throes of moving out of the mission home, so some logistical concerns had to be dealt with. Joel was able to go to work for his brother, who owned a small copier-rental business. This provided a monthly income, but it was about 30 percent less than we had been receiving as missionaries, so it was going to be a challenge to live on. I don't know what I would have done without my family who were living close by at the time. God provided the help we needed physically during an excruciating, emotional time. It is strange to realize the therapy that painting a house with my dad could provide, or the emotional boost of having good friends show up with trucks to move furniture.

One Loss Leads to Another

We faced the incredible hurt and ostracism of our own church in a new way in this part of our journey. Only one adult genuinely offered his help and actually showed up to follow through on that offer. It seemed to us that the rest of the church body did their best to avoid us. We felt very keenly what

David had spoken of in Psalms 55:12-14: "If an enemy were insulting me, I could endure it; if a foe were rising against me, I could hide. But it is you, a man like myself, my companion, my close friend, with whom I once enjoyed sweet fellowship at the house of God" (NLT). This kind of hurt cuts deeply.

We were very aware that many of the individuals in the church felt helpless to know what to do in our situation. They did not want to do anything outside of what the leadership of the church had stipulated for us. This meant that although we'd been members of the church for over fourteen years, we had many good friends who felt powerless to reach out to us.

Joel had developed deep relationships with several of the guys in the youth group, some high schoolers and some college age. He had been told by the elders of the church to have no further contact with these guys. But this was very hard to do, since these young men were determined to show their love and support to Joel and our family and kept coming by our house to visit or offer help.

On the day that we moved Josh, a young college student, arrived with his truck to help, and so did two other young guys, Jared and Jarred. Interestingly, these were the same two that had cleaned up our house after the police search. Most of our friends from our church kept their distance, but these guys whom we had been told to stay away from had come of their own volition and insisted on helping. We were grateful for their love and concern and the physical display of that in their willingness to work. I do not know how we would have moved without them. Again, God was showing us His faithfulness and love.

People in American Christian culture today do not know how to deal with messy sins. Often this leads to an epidemic I refer to as "plastic people." No one wants to admit what they truly struggle with for fear of the shockwaves that might ripple through the entire church. So instead of admitting our sins to one another as we are commanded to in Scripture, we hide them. We pretend that everything is fine. Our struggles with sinful behaviors and addictions are tucked away where no one can see, or they are made light of. The ironic thing is that this treatment of sin often leads to the trap of more sin. People who do not confess their sins to one another are often stuck in a cycle of repetition.

However, our church's inability to handle the open nature of Joel's heinous sins is a prime reason why people remain so private about their struggles. And having seen what the church did to us, no one in our church who was struggling with the sin of pornography would have felt the slightest encouragement to seek help. On the contrary, they would have been more likely to dig deeper into their own clandestine pit. Joel had certainly struggled for a long time without success against the temptation of pornography; he had struggled alone, asking God for forgiveness and begging God to help him change, but inevitably failing.

God has created the body of Christ to function together as a body. Joel did not have support, encouragement, or rebuke from other Christians because he kept his sinful patterns a secret. Once these sins were laid out for the world to see, many of those who did have the opportunity to form that kind of corrective, supportive community around Joel failed to do so.

The Illusive Comfort of the Greater Good

During this time, my journal filled up with questions and prayers for God to comfort, give grace, and even rescue us. I found comfort in the Psalms and even in the story of Job. I will never forget the beautiful assurance my sister Tammy offered me in one of my darker moments: "Tabitha, we can let go of God, but He never lets go of us." I had come to the end of myself and my ability to convince myself of any good. And at that end, God was hanging onto me.

In August, two months into the waiting, I wrote this in my journal:

> I feel spent, emotionally, physically, and spiritually. Doing everything the best I can isn't enough…some days I'd rather be dead than to keep dragging on through these unknown waters alone.

I was still searching God's Word for answers, referring to this period as my forty-year desert, and closed this entry with, "In the end, God was merciful to Job, 'For the Lord is full of tenderness and mercy' (James 5:11). Be merciful to me, O Lord. My heart waits for you."

Often when we are in the midst of suffering, especially in a holding pattern, we want to make some sense of our situation, erroneously assuming that this will provide the comfort we long for. I longed to know that some good would come out of the raw pain I was experiencing. Jerry Sittser commented that no matter what positive impact his book about his family's experience had on other people, it would not mitigate the pain of their loss. He says, "My suffering is as puzzling and horrible to me now as it was the day it happened. The good that may come out of the loss does not erase its badness or excuse the wrong done. Nothing can do that." Nothing can erase the pain. Desperately grasping for meaning often leads to further disillusionment, rather can comfort.

If we truly value God's glory above our own personal comfort, then maybe end results would be a comfort, without trivializing the pain. But most of the time, we do not value God's honor or His glory over ourselves. So knowing the outcome does not assuage the pain, because it cannot justify the pain in our one-dimensional economy of equality. The reality is we cannot appreciate the impact of the bigger picture.

Many of us know the story of Horatio Spafford, the author of the well-known hymn, "It Is Well with My Soul." After losing his four daughters at sea on a crossing to England from America, he traveled to England to meet up with his wife. When he was told by the captain of the ship that they were sailing over the place where the ship carrying his family had gone down, Spafford stood on deck and wrote the first verse of the song. If Spafford had known the impact this song would have on millions of Christians through the centuries, would this have made the pain of losing his children any less keen? Would he have felt that the death of his children was a worthy sacrifice for the glory of God? We can only guess at what he would have felt. Surely, the grief of missing his daughters would still have been evident in his life. But the simple truth is that unless we value God above our personal solace, knowing His glory sometimes comes out of our pain offers little or no comfort. But, and this is crucial, when we truly find our deepest desire is knowing God, then whatever He does in our pain brings us comfort, because we know it is good.

Waiting Patiently in this Life

Prolonged waits here on earth tend to turn our eyes heavenward. I found myself longing for eternity with a renewed fervor as I contemplated the impending consequences in our future. Even though looking forward to eternity is a good thing, it can keep us from actually accepting and dealing with the time we have here on earth. David wrote in Psalms 27:13-14, "I remain confident in this: I will see the goodness of the Lord in the land of the living. Wait for the Lord; be strong, and take heart, and wait for the Lord" (NIV). These verses were a great reminder to me that while eternity is truly something to look forward to, my time on earth is a unique opportunity for seeing God's goodness. David was certain of God's hand in action "in this life." He was not resigned to disaster now because in heaven everything would be better. So while I found myself longing for eternity, I also clung to the promises of God for my time in this world.

In no way do I want to imply that having a heavenly perspective is a negative thing. One of the obvious goods that comes from suffering is the turning of our eyes away from security on this earth and toward our final destiny. The psalmist cried out to God, "Turn away my eyes from looking at worthless things, and revive me in Your way" (Psalms 119: 37, NKJV). Suffering is one of the tools that God uses to do just that. When we can look at our suffering here on earth in light of the beauty of heaven with our Savior, we will be revived. No amount of comfort in this world can equal what awaits us in heaven.

My caution is that we not reconcile ourselves to misery here. The stark contrast of sin to grace in this life provides a platform for the exposure of God's glory in and through our painful circumstances. Even though heaven will be far beyond anything we can imagine, and the anticipation of that is a great comfort, God's miraculous work in our lives here on earth will not disappoint if we wait patiently for Him.

The Miracle of Walking and Not Fainting

Waiting can wear us out. There is no other way to put it. Isaiah 40:31 says, "They that wait upon the Lord will renew their strength; they will mount up with wings as eagles. They will run and not get weary; they will walk and not faint" (NKJV). Through the long months that Joel and I waited to hear from the legal authorities, there were many days when I felt totally spent by the waiting. But God reminds us that when we wait on Him, instead of waiting for a change in our circumstances, our strength will be renewed. Joel and I experienced this truth in a new way during this time. We began to expect God's entrance into the difficult areas of our lives and to wait for Him to grow us toward each other and toward Him.

Soaring like eagles is obviously a miraculous event. Running without becoming exhausted is also noteworthy. But walking and not fainting sounds just a little commonplace. When we are in the intense heat of a difficult situation or the fresh throes of a tragedy, God's provision and presence are intensely real. But when the suffering drags on for a long period, we begin to realize that walking without fainting certainly takes an act of God just the same as soaring with eagles. Joel and I were finding that walking without fainting required a constant reliance on God.

Since our home church had asked Joel not to attend services, we bounced around for a while on Sundays, visiting one church after another and never really feeling like we belonged. It was hard to imagine jumping into a new church relationship in the state we were in, and if our own home church found us too risky to interact with, then what would other churches think? Of course, not telling anyone was always an option, but that left us feeling disconnected and deceitful. We did not see our friends from our home church any more either, except for the occasional visit from one of the youth-group guys who insisted on stopping in even though they were not supposed to.

After several months of awkward and frustrating Sunday mornings, we visited my sisters' church. It was small and very different from what we were used to. But the people were warm, inviting, and genuine.

The depth of spirituality was compelling, and we loved being with our family on a Sunday morning. We began to attend regularly, gradually getting to know people. At first we did not say anything about what was going in our lives. But eventually Joel decided it was necessary to make the pastor aware of our situation and the investigation. The grace he extended was refreshing and therapeutic, and we knew God had us in the right fellowship of believers for this time in our lives.

Later as we shared with our new church family about the pending investigation, we were received with kind and gracious forgiveness. God's love spread in the heart of these believers and overflowed to us, offering healing to our hurting hearts.

We attempted to use our "desert" time wisely, going to counseling together, spending long hours with each other and doing special things with the kids.

When the leaders of our old home church realized how long the wait might be before Joel knew anything about his case, they decided to invite him to join the men's Bible study group that met every Tuesday night. They felt it would be a safe first step in allowing him to return to that community of believers. Joel attended this study regularly with his dad. He confessed his past and asked for their support, which they graciously gave. This was a very therapeutic experience for Joel. His honesty with the guys helped him to feel less afraid and less of an outcast. Many of the men from that study showed up to support us on the day of the sentencing hearing.

We also spent time with our extended family and talked about possible future scenarios. But even as we did all these things, we begged God to let this cup pass. We prayed fervently that by some miracle, the consequences that Joel faced would be averted. At times I felt desperate, pleading with God to keep my family together. I could not fathom living on my own, raising my kids alone, and being without Joel. And I could not imagine what life would be like for him in prison either.

Most of the time, no matter how much we tried to be prepared, we could not really face the future objectively. One thing we were learning, however, was how desperately we needed God, no matter what the future would hold.

Months dragged by. September came and went. Joel struggled to work enough to pay the bills, and I took house-cleaning jobs now and then to fill in the gaps. The kids settled into school, and we all adjusted to the routine. Life was almost normal. But I knew it was only the eye of the storm, the calm in-between.

In November I wrote this note to God:

> Some days feel so routine, normal, and yet I know we're still in the eye of the storm and have yet to endure the other half of its fury. For this reason, I constantly beg you, Father, let the storm abate! And yet whatever happens, help me to keep my eyes on you. I need you every moment, lest I be drowned in the panic of unknown waters.

My own comfort and relief meant so much to me in this time that I had to beg God to give me a desire for Him that would override my other emotions.

I have never been a patient person. Waiting does not come naturally to the average human. God knows that; therefore, He riddled Scripture with stories about waiting, commands to wait, and examples of what waiting demonstrates and produces.

Noah is one great example of the demonstration of trust in waiting. He built an ark and waited one hundred and twenty years for God to send the promised rain. Many historians and commentators think that the earth had not received rain prior to the flood. So God's revelation that He was going to flood the earth with water from the sky must have sounded farfetched. But Noah obediently prepared for this event, trusting that if God said it would happen, it surely would. When the rain finally did come, Noah and his family found themselves trapped in that ark, adrift in the floodwaters for more than a year! Each phase of his journey included waiting.

Caleb and Joshua gave a glowing report of the promised land. Their hearts were right before God. And yet both of them were doomed to wait along with the rest of Israel for forty years in the wilderness before they could move in and possess the land, all because the other ten spies rebelled! They had argued vehemently with the people, begging them to see God's hand and provision in giving the land of Canaan to Israel. They had openly rejected the fear of the other ten spies. Caleb and Joshua had behaved admirably in the face of intense peer pressure. They were right! But none of this meant they got to enjoy the land immediately. Instead, through no fault of their own, they were forced to endure forty years in the desert. Talk about agony in waiting, yet nowhere in Scripture do we find either of them complaining or growing bitter. When the forty-year wait was up and everyone else their age was dead, God used them both mightily in routing the wicked nations settled in Canaan and claiming the promised land for Israel. This story is a beautiful example of God's power unleashed in those who wait on Him.

David was anointed king and waited for years to see that promise fulfilled. In the meantime, he was pursued and harassed by half-crazed King Saul, who sought to take his life. David did not have an easy wait at all, but at least he was kept busy!

Mary, the mother of Jesus, was given a beautiful and painful prophecy by Simeon when Jesus was only eight days old. "This child is destined to cause many in Israel to fall, but he will be a joy to many others...And a sword will pierce your very soul," Simeon told Mary. She waited over thirty years, wondering at the impending agony that Simeon had predicted.

One of the reasons that I have so much trouble waiting is that I fail to see the value in it. I am a person of action. I want to see things getting done. And if something difficult has to happen, then let's just get it over with. What gets done in waiting? Often, since the results of waiting are not measurable, it can seem like nothing gets done. Clearly God does not see it that way. The value in waiting is this: God reveals Himself to us in the waiting in ways we could never otherwise know Him, because it reminds us of how little control we actually have.

I love what Psalms 130:5 says: "I wait for the Lord, my whole being waits, and in His Word I put my hope" (NIV). The psalmist vividly describes what it feels like to wait. His whole being is involved, and his entire hope is in God alone. Waiting puts me in a position of vulnerability which throws me at the feet of Christ.

God was not silent in our waiting. He was at work in Joel and me, individually and as a couple. During those long days, weeks, and months of waiting, we began to seek God with a new desperation and to find Him in unexpected ways. Walking without fainting may have once seemed mundane; now it truly became the miracle of our everyday lives.

In the Waiting

Let me find you in the waiting,

Let me seek your face alone,

My whole being waits for you,

I lie prostrate at your throne.

Let me find you in the waiting,

O, Lord, I'm desperate and afraid,

My hope is in you, my God,

On you my mind is stayed.

Let me find you in the waiting,

When I can't see left from right,

When I see so little worth,

And I finally give up the fight.

Let me find you in the waiting,

Surrendered to your will.

Confident of your work,

I hear you whisper, "Peace, be still."

FREEDOM IN FORGIVENESS

No Way Out, Only Through

Shortly after we got married in the summer of 1993, Joel and I both worked for the same company. We drove to work together, saw each other around the office, and drove home together. One of our friends and coworkers commented that they did not know how we could put up with each other for that much of the time. Both Joel and I were confounded by that idea. We thought it a real blessing to be able to spend most of our days together. We never tired of each other's company.

During our first couple years of marriage, we were in Bible college together. Then I continued in school to pursue my bachelor's degree in education, and Joel began to work full-time so we could pay the college bills. Joel worked long hours, and we rarely had spending money because we were committed to my getting through college without having a huge debt.

To others, it may have seemed as if Joel were supporting my goals and college aspirations. But we saw things quite differently. We both considered my education as a part of our calling as a family. We worked toward that goal in different ways. But it was our desire, our calling, not mine or his.

Tabitha Joy Price

Joel and I often felt like we had it too easy. We did not face many of the struggles we saw other couples deal with. And even when we did go through frustrations and difficult circumstances, they only drew us closer together as a couple.

On top of all that, Joel and I had made a firm commitment to each other and before the Lord that divorce was not an option for us. From the moment of our engagement, we knew there was no turning back, no way out. We were committed to looking for a way through, not out—no matter what came our way.

Because of this foundation in our marriage, Joel knew that even when I found out about his hidden obsession, I would not leave him.

Joel wrote later about the effect of faithfulness and forgiveness in his life during this time:

> Never once did I doubt that Tabitha would forgive me and stand by my side through the difficulties to come. Our song when we dated in high school was Russ Taff's "This Love Is Strong." Of course, we could never have envisioned then how I would test that commitment we had made to each other or the commitment to "for better or for worse." I did not know I would be the cause of the "worse." I did not start out our marriage with the intent of causing the woman I love immeasurable pain. The fact that I knew she would never leave me never felt like a license to cause her grief. I never thought, "Well, she will never leave me, so…" I can honestly say that there is only one thing in my life that could cause

82

me more anguish than losing Tabitha. That one thing, I discovered, is exactly what happened. I hurt her more than I will ever know. Holding her while she sobbed, knowing I was the cause and feeling powerless to be the cure, was far worse torture than I could ever have imagined.

I thought it would have been so much easier if she didn't love me enough to stay. She could leave and isolate herself from the pain I was causing. Sometimes I reasoned it would be easier if I were to die. "How can I remove myself from her life with the least amount of pain?" was my question. Maybe an "accident." That would certainly be easier for me. But I knew how much she loved me. I couldn't do it to her. I loved her more than the release of death.

Her faithfulness to me never provided me with a license to sin. The fact of the matter is this: I believed a lie. This completely tainted my perspective. I believed the lie so completely that my actions reflected them. Imagine this scenario: I hand you a gun as a prop in a movie we are filming. I assure you that it has no bullets in it, and it is not even a real gun. I then proceed to tell you to point it at a costar, someone you care about in real life, and I tell you to pull the trigger. In exchange for this, you will receive a huge paycheck. Doubtless, you will not think there is any risk in following through with this arrangement. You would likely go ahead and pull the trigger. But guess what, the gun is actually real and is loaded!

My sinful choices had so deceived me that this was the reasoning I used to excuse my Internet activity. Digital images on a computer screen are not real; they are just make-believe. How can something make-believe be dangerous? Besides, no one will ever find out. In my mind, I wasn't choosing my sin over my wife's happiness. I had convinced myself that the two could coexist. And isn't that the lie we all tell ourselves about sin? It's not as bad as it seems, and it doesn't have to affect the rest of our lives. The poison of sin is that it inoculates us against the symptoms while the disease destroys.[iv]

When Joel confessed his sinful choices to me, I was too hurt to be angry. But I also knew I would never leave him. As much as it hurt, I loved him, and I could not even imagine life without him. Nothing would be better about a life that didn't include him, not for me, not for the kids. And beyond that, I knew for certain that God intended for us to stay together. Having that confidence, I knew that I had to forgive Joel.

Barriers to Overcome

Standing by Joel and supporting him through this incredible trial would be impossible if I refused to forgive him. And the process of restoration would be undermined if I allowed resentment to grow by failing to extend forgiveness. If I were going to support him through this trial, forgiveness was not an option; it was an imperative.

However, no matter how necessary I knew forgiveness to be, it could only come through the work of my heavenly Father in my life. I loved Joel, I knew he was repentant, and I wanted to forgive him, but my emotions did not necessarily follow that desire.

One obvious concern when it comes to forgiveness is that the person being forgiven will not take seriously the damage they have done. I knew Joel took seriously the agony he was causing me, but others did not seem to see that in Joel as quickly, and I feared that my choice to forgive would be viewed somewhat like an ostrich sticking its head in the sand. It might appear that I was in denial, refusing to accept the significance of the issue. Some might even think I was justifying Joel's behavior. I also feared that people might think of me as weak. They might see my choice to forgive Joel as acquiescence to avoid the upheaval of leaving. I didn't want to appear weak, or ignorant, or deceived.

Slowly I began to realize that all those concerns were based on my own assessment. They were a "might," not an absolute, and they all revolved around what people would think of me. God was again dealing with my heart in the area of pride. He wanted me to forgive and offer His grace, no matter what others might think or say about it. I had to relinquish my fears, abandon myself to God and His care, and allow the forgiveness He shed in my heart to be genuine and complete.

Another obstacle that impedes forgiveness in the human heart is a lack of understanding of sin. We love to categorize sin because it helps us feel better about the sins we allow in our own lives. It is true that sins have varying degrees of consequences; what is not true is that they have varying degrees of wickedness. Adam and Eve ate a piece of fruit, disobeying a command of God. They were not brutal to the animals; they did not murder one another. They did not rape, abuse, or pillage. They disobeyed God and did what they wanted. And because of that, death entered the human race.

Every time we disobey God, our sin is enough to send us to hell. Every single nasty thought, angry exclamation, and selfish act that we commit is enough to cost Jesus His life on the cross. It makes us feel solvent and sanitary to categorize sin. We consider those who have committed gross sins to be more guilty than we are. But that is a lie of sin within us, and it leads to more death and destruction.

One day God said to me, "Tabitha, your pride stinks just as much as Joel's sins. Your pride caused my Son's death on the cross. It is repulsive, disgusting, and heinous to me, just like Joel's sins." This rebuke left me reeling. I was horrified to realize that my selfish pride was a constant cause of grief to my Savior. Joel's sin was more socially abhorrent, but both of us were equally guilty before a holy God. I was challenged again with my responsibility to forgive Joel. That forgiveness is based on my belief and understanding that God through Christ has forgiven me an incredible debt that I could not otherwise pay.

Unforgiven Debts

Jesus told a compelling parable to demonstrate this point in the gospel of Matthew. A man who owed his lord a huge sum of money was brought before this master for not having paid back his debt. The master decreed that he and his family be sold as slaves and all his goods sold as well in order to pay back the debt. The debtor began to beg for mercy, promising to get the money somehow and crying out for just a little more time. The master had compassion on him and forgave him the debt. He didn't give him another deadline for paying it off; he cancelled it altogether. The debtor was overcome by his lord's gracious gift and thanked him profusely.

But when he left, he went and found a guy who owed him a small sum. The difference between the debt he'd just been forgiven and the debt owed him by this guy was probably roughly the difference between a year's wage and a lifetime of wages. But the recently forgiven debtor grabbed the other guy by the throat and began demanding payment. He was deaf to the cries for mercy and refused to give him any more time to pay his debt. Instead he had the guy thrown in jail until he paid back the debt. Meanwhile some of the master's servants witnessed this event. They went back to the master and relayed to him what had happened. The master was rightfully appalled. He was disgusted by the greedy actions of the forgiven servant. In a rage, he called back the servant and demanded that he be imprisoned until he paid back every cent of the debt that had been cancelled.

This man had the chance at a new life. His wife and kids were rescued from being sold into servitude, because of the gracious forgiveness of the master. He could have experienced such joy. He missed out on so much by refusing to live in the joy of that forgiveness, by refusing to pass it on.

If only the man who had been forgiven so much had really understood and appreciated that gift, things could have been so different. Imagine this: The forgiven slave went on his way, skipping, and singing. He could hardly wait to get home and tell his wife of the wonderful gift of grace and forgiveness he had received from the master. Suddenly the forgiven man remembered the money his neighbor owed him and had been unable to repay. With a great burst of energy, he ran to his neighbor's house to share the great news. Since I no longer have to pay my debt, I can forgive him his! He thought.

When his neighbor came to the door, he exclaimed, "You'll never guess what happened to me today! The master forgave the huge debt I owed him! I thought I was headed to debtor's prison for sure. But instead I'm on my way home to share this incredible news with my wife! Do you know what this means?"

The nervous neighbor shook his head, hoping that maybe he had forgotten about the debt. "This means you don't have to pay me back that money you owed me! If the master can forgive me the huge debt I owed him, then the least I can do is forgive you the pithy sum you owe me. I am so happy to be able to free you of that debt. Isn't it wonderful?" Amid all the gushing, the neighbor began to cry. He had expected such a different scene. He was overwhelmed by the kindness shown to him by his neighbor.

There was dancing and laughter and a huge block party to celebrate the freedom both men experienced. The forgiven man got to experience a small piece of the joy that his master had felt at forgiving him. In receiving that forgiveness and passing it on, he had received a double blessing.

Of course this is not the ending Jesus told, but it is worth considering because it reminds us of what can happen when we do forgive. I am the debtor in this story, and every time I hold a grudge against someone else, I am denying the power of Christ's forgiveness of me. Not only that, I am refusing myself the joy that comes with sharing in Christ's forgiveness.

Convincing Our Emotions

A final reason we withhold forgiveness is because our emotional pain keeps us from being willing to forgive. It is textbook teaching to say that we should forgive. It is quite another thing to actually choose forgiveness when our agony is deep and raw. Corrie ten Boom tells the story of meeting one of the SS officers who had stood guard over her during her humiliating and tormenting saga in Nazi prison. He came up to her after a service in which she had spoken on forgiveness. He did not recognize her, but of course she recognized him. When he reached out his hand to shake hers, speaking enthusiastically about how amazing God's forgiveness is, she froze.

This is what she had to say about that event: "His hand was thrust out to shake mine. And I, who had preached so often to the people in Bloemendaal the need to forgive, kept my hand at my side. Even as the angry, vengeful thoughts boiled through me, I saw the sin of them. Jesus Christ had died for this man; was I going to ask for more? 'Lord Jesus,' I prayed, 'forgive me and help me to forgive him.' I tried to smile; I struggled to raise my hand. I could not. I felt nothing, not the slightest spark of warmth or charity.

"And so again I breathed a silent prayer. 'Jesus, I cannot forgive him. Give me your forgiveness.' As I took his hand, the most incredible thing happened. From my shoulder along my arm and through my hand, a current seemed to pass from me to him, while into my heart sprang a love for this stranger that almost overwhelmed me. And so I discovered that it is not on our forgiveness any more than on our goodness that the world's healing hinges, but on His. When He tells us to love our enemies, He gives, along with the command, the love itself."[v]

God's forgiveness is supernatural. It is not something we can conjure up on our own. But when we submit to Him and allow His forgiveness to be shed in our heart and extended to those who have hurt us deeply, it is a testimony to His greatness. It gives glory to His name. Corrie ten Boom showed that God was as good as she had claimed by the way she lived. She exemplified Jesus and His forgiveness by allowing it to flow through her.

Forgiving Joel was not hard work on my part. It was a choice to submit to the work of Christ in my heart. His Holy Spirit did something supernatural in me, just as Corrie testified to. And I found that with the forgiveness came a deeper love and a strong desire for Joel to know my heart was truly tender toward him.

Living Out Forgiveness

It was the evening after the horrific phone call in the dentist's office, and Joel and I were preparing for bed in the basement room my brother had set up for our visit. Joel was tentative toward me, knowing the pain was raw and I had not processed most of what had gone on that day. I knew in my heart that no matter what we would face, we would need to face it together in order to survive. I did not want to impede the process of healing by leaving Joel to wonder if I would punish him for his sin.

Because Joel's sin was an immoral choice that violated the purity of our marriage, I also needed to live out my forgiveness to him by not withholding intimacy in our relationship. As we crawled into bed, I whispered to him, "I want you to know that I forgive you, and I won't hold this against you or over your head for the rest of our life." We held each other and wept. Our time together was painfully precious as we experienced God's grace drawing us closer through the ragged agony.

I had seen the damage a grudging form of forgiveness can do to a marriage. And I knew I did not want that for us. I knew that in forgiving Joel, I was also doing myself a favor and saving us both heartache.

But this also meant not recanting on my forgiveness and not expecting Joel to make it up to me in some way. Of course that is the natural human tendency, so I found myself in a place of desperately needing God to work out that forgiveness in my everyday life and actions.

Shortly after our return to Florida, we met with some of our closest friends and told them the whole story. Donna, one of my dearest friends for more than fifteen years, held my hands and earnestly asked, "Oh, Tabitha, is there anything I can do?"

My response was heartfelt. "Forgive Joel. Love him, and don't hold this against him. I have forgiven him, and I need you to as well."

I could not stand the hurt Joel had already brought on himself and others. And I longed to protect him from further pain. I knew that our relationship with these dear friends was being tested in deep and raging waters. Would they be so repulsed by Joel's sin that they would pull away from us? They had a young teenage daughter. Would they feel concern for her and wonder if Joel were a possible threat? Of course, I knew that would be an understandable response. But if they were unable to forgive Joel and live out that forgiveness in their interactions with him, our relationship with them would suffer. What a relief for me when Donna reassured me that Joel had her forgiveness. During the long months of waiting, these friends lived out that forgiveness toward us. They spent time in our home and never treated Joel as suspect.

Forgiveness and Trust

Forgiving Joel has been a step of this journey that God has worked out in my life in a powerful way. But I have often struggled with how to live out that forgiveness to Joel while not fully trusting him. Is it wrong not to trust him? Is "forgive and forget" possible?

Truthfully, "forgive and forget" is not merely a simplistic view of forgiveness; it is a potentially destructive one. Forgiving someone is not holding a charge against them. It is releasing them from the debt they owed. Forgetting that they ever owed a debt diminishes the act of forgiveness. Forgetting the offense does not deepen the relationship, because the honest truth is we do not really forget; we just push it to the recesses of our mind and pretend to forget. If forgetting were truly possible, it still would not be the wisest course of action for the relationship. Part of the forgiveness I offer Joel is out of a desire to lovingly draw him away from the temptation to sin again. If I forget or ignore that he ever had a problem, then I am not going to be much help in his areas of weakness.

What is true about the old adage is that once we forgive, we cannot beat the person over the head with the debt they no longer owe. A forgiving spirit does not go around constantly reminding the person that they have been forgiven. Nor does it look for retribution. True forgiveness does include forgetting any ideas about personal gain.

Trust is something that takes time to build. It is not something that is gained immediately in a relationship, nor is it something that can be quickly restored. Joel and I had a deep foundation of trust in our marriage that was built over years of sharing truthfully with each other. When Joel decided to embark on his secret and sinful journey, he stepped off the path of honesty and destroyed that foundation of trust.

Joel has come to understand this and has accepted it as his most painful consequence. To beat Joel over the head with the "you can't be trusted" stick would certainly not be in keeping with the forgiveness I have offered him. On the other hand, to completely trust him again would be destructive in the same way that allowing a two-year-old to swim alone is. No loving parent allows his toddler the freedom to hop into the pool on his own and swim laps. Even if the little guy can swim, it is just not a safe environment to face alone at that age.

Joel calls himself "untrustworthy." He has shared in depth the pain he lives with, knowing that he cannot be trusted. Joel wrote this about the subject of trust:

> I know in many ways that my dishonesty is what hurt Tabitha the most. The deception caused incalculable damage. Honesty and trust are fundamental in any Godly relationship. We knew that, and it was the foundation of our marriage. We both had the expectation of transparency from each other and no keeping secrets. So why had I chosen to walk down a path that would lead me away from transparency and truthfulness in our relationship? Why had I not chosen to be honest with her about my struggle? I have always had confidence in her commitment to love me unconditionally, flaws and all. I knew she wouldn't leave me. I had kept my secret, because that was part of the drive that made my quest so powerful and heady. The deception of my wife and everyone I cared about

was not only necessary so that I could continue my love affair with pornography, but the secrecy itself became an increasingly dominant part of the allure. I lied to myself, believing the deception to be worth the risk.

I know that Christ has forgiven me and there is "now no condemnation in Him." Because of that, I can forgive myself and my family can and has forgiven me. But, I can never fully trust myself again and neither should anyone else. Just as an alcoholic cannot be trusted to hang out in a bar, I cannot be trusted with the Internet. It is a demonstration of love on my family's part to hold me accountable in this area.

It is my hope that in most areas of my life, I will regain my family's trust, because for me, the trust I've lost is the consequence that stings the worst, much more by far than my prison sentence. I never truly valued people's trust before I deprived myself of it, possibly for the rest of my life.[vi]

Over time, Joel will rebuild some of that trust. As he walks before man in submission to his Savior, the people he loves will see that and begin to trust him again. In the meantime, we will lovingly hold him accountable. As his wife, I will be honest with my fears and straightforward with my questions. But as a result of forgiveness, I will not badger him or expect him to choose the path of evil. "Love never gives up...is always hopeful and endures through every circumstance" (1 Corinthians 13:7, NLT). Our family will expect him to make wise and faithful choices.

Freedom in Forgiveness

As God worked out His forgiveness in my heart, I experienced a deep and abiding freedom. I did not have to make sure Joel did anything to atone for his sin. I did not have to judge the genuineness of his repentance, although it was readily apparent. Instead, I was given the blessing of loving someone whom others might find unlovable; the blessing of supporting someone in desperate need; and the blessing of sharing in God's story of redemption.

The only basis for true forgiveness is unconditional love. Our Savior has chosen to love us not for what we do or how we behave. He has chosen to love us because of who He is. That makes His love for us unconditional. Joel and I have experienced this unconditional love in our lives. Even when Joel may have felt he deserved much less, he knew what he would receive: God's unceasing love. God's love so freely given to us is what spurs us on to extend forgiveness to others.

The end of the parable Jesus told about the unforgiving servant is a picture of justice. The man who refused to forgive a small debt after being forgiven a much larger one was dragged back before his master and required to pay every penny of the astronomical debt he owed. He was thrown into prison until the debt could be paid, which implied a life sentence for him since the debt was so huge.

What did Jesus mean by giving the parable this ending? The man ended up receiving justice for his actions, not mercy. I think Jesus is showing us exactly what we deserve. Every single one of us has been the unforgiving servant. Every time we sin, we are mocking the sacrifice Christ paid to forgive our debt of sin. Even when we know we ourselves need mercy, we do not extend mercy. Justice would call for an ending like that of the parable. But Jesus's unconditional love calls for mercy. His unconditional love is what compels us to live differently, to forsake the path of self-righteousness, and to embark on the path of humility and mercy.

Forgiveness is costly. To truly forgive, we have to relinquish our right to punish. We have to extend grace, treating someone in ways they do not deserve to be treated.

But I was learning by God's grace that withholding forgiveness is also very costly. Grudging forgiveness is the seed to bitterness, and once a root of bitterness has taken hold, the damage is inestimable. I knew I didn't want that for Joel and me. God reminded me that no matter how good it might feel at the moment to withhold forgiveness, in the long run, the consequences would be devastating for us both.

Through the experience of forgiving Joel, I have begun to understand in the tiniest measure how much it cost my Savior to forgive me. How humbling and powerful! I have been a believer for over thirty years, but it took my present pain to open my eyes to the incredible cost of forgiveness. It was not the physical agony of the cross alone, it was the spiritual agony of seeing me distant and apathetic to Him, and yet loving me enough that even though my sin was completely repulsive, He longed to reach me.

Oswald Chambers put it this way: "Once you realize all that it cost God to forgive you, you will be held as in a vise, constrained by the love of God."[vii] There is no amount of obligation to a written code that can equal the compulsion of understanding His love and forgiveness.

INCREASED CAPACITY

The Storm Intensifies

On December 18, nearly six months after the initial warrant and interview, we rushed out the door for school and were met by half a dozen black vehicles and armed federal agents. We had been assured previously by the police officer in charge of the case that this would not happen. She had told us that because of Joel's honesty and cooperation, he would be ordered to turn himself in when the evidence proved to be enough for an arrest. So this was a complete shock. Of course, six months of hearing nothing had also fueled our hopes that maybe the call would never come.

It was as if icy water followed by hot coals had been thrown in my face as I took in the scene of my husband's arrest. I had the presence of mind to usher the boys back into the house, where I made them sit and wait in stunned silence. I then rushed back outside, begging to know the charges and where they were taking him. Joel told me where to find the lawyer's phone number and to call him right away. After Joel was handcuffed, with tears rolling down his anguished face, they let me kiss him good-bye. It was the most agonizing moment I had ever had to face. In a surreal moment, I realized that these people standing around in my yard, treating my husband as a dangerous man, had no concept of who we really were. Again, I felt the anguish of a ruined reputation. Thus began the most excruciating and longest day of my life to date.

I was desolate, and as I reentered the house, I could hear the panicked sobs of Jaden. Marshall sat next to him, with tears silently trickling down his cheeks.

I will never know how, but we made it through that first hour of uncertain agony. I called Tammy, my sister and best friend, immediately. She was right down the road on her way to the meeting spot for a ride to school, so she arrived in short order. I also called my parents and younger sister, Dar, all of whom came right away. So I was surrounded by loving, caring family in a matter of minutes.

But none of us knew what to do besides calling the lawyer. A strange emptiness and helplessness pervaded. I was relieved that both boys decided they wanted to go ahead to school, because I did not know what I would do with them all day waiting and wondering. One of my close friends was Marshall's teacher, and my grandma was Jaden's teacher, so I knew they would have the loving support they needed.

The day of Joel's arrest was our first knowledge of the case having been turned over to the federal court. When I contacted the lawyer that Joel had previously consulted, he was not only brusque on the phone but refused to take the case because it had gone federal. But he did give me a very important piece of information—a referral to a lawyer in Orlando who did take federal cases.

My day was filled with obtaining a lawyer and preparing to be at the courthouse by 3:00 p.m. for the bond hearing Joel was to receive. My family jumped to my aid. With little funds of my own, I did not know how I would secure a lawyer. But Joel's parents offered the financial aid immediately. And even as my brain felt like mush, God enabled me to make wise decisions.

The hearing brought additional agony as the prosecution described pictures and videos of a very graphic nature that had been found on Joel's hard drives. I actually knew physical pain as my heart broke. Joel was clearly broken. I longed to hold him and cry together.

At the same time, I was repulsed and horrified at the secret compulsion that had been a part of my beloved husband's life and was now so boldly exposed. Questions flew through my mind. How could they be saying these things about the man I loved, the man I was married to and committed to for life? I knew him better than this! Yet the look on his face, and previous admissions to me, let me know these accusations were accurate. I loved him still, but I wondered if he might be broken beyond my ability to help. Finding myself helpless to change my circumstances and helpless to change my husband was excruciating, yet strangely freeing. It released me from a self-imposed responsibility and threw me at the mercy of a loving and trustworthy God.

The lawyer I had retained was wise, honest, and kind. The judge in Joel's bond hearing was fair-minded and objective. Before we had arrived at the courthouse, the lawyer had called me to tell me the prosecution was requesting that Joel be remanded without bond. This would mean that he would be held in county jail until his trial, which could take weeks or even months. This seemed absurd to me; this was the kind of treatment that should be reserved for dangerous criminals. I could not make myself understand that they viewed my husband as just that, a dangerous criminal! Our lawyer explained to me that because of our international travels, the prosecution was suggesting that Joel had been involved in sex tourism, implying that the only reason he had been in Venezuela was for some clandestine life of sexual promiscuity. They also claimed he had thousands of suspicious files on his computer and hard drive, and that he had participated in distributing illegal files. I was horrified at the accusations the prosecution threw at my husband. I knew it was true that he indeed had illegal files of child pornography on the computer—how many, neither of us knew for sure—but the other accusations of sex tourism and distribution were stretches of sketchy information in an effort to malign him further.

Our lawyer, of course, had had little time to prepare any sort of defense but was well-seasoned in criminal law. He also believed me immediately when I told him of our ministry in Venezuela, and asked if I would be willing to testify regarding our travels and the reasons for them, which, of course, I felt compelled to do. He felt like the prosecution's accusations were the unfortunate results of years of investigating sex crimes. In the prosecution's mind, a person with illegal files of child pornography, on his computer is an automatic risk to all children and even to society in general.

Finally, after what seemed like an eternity of debate, Joel was released to home confinement instead of being sent to county jail. The security guard who escorted us from the courthouse told us how "lucky" we had been. "You got the only judge in the district who would release to home confinement on a case like this," he told us.

"Lots of people were praying," I assured him. I knew no luck had been involved. The sovereign hand of my Savior and Lord had moved on our behalf to arrange just the right judge and the right lawyer. My faith was bolstered by this obvious intervention.

Major Adjustments

Joel and I entered a new dimension of waiting. New rules of home confinement governed our lives. More questions both involving his crime and legal issues had to be openly discussed. We could no longer hope that the problem might just disappear and never resurface. The black band around Joel's ankle was a stark, daily reminder of impending loss. At first I could not look at it without feeling sick. The bold physical reminder of all that we had lost was almost too much to bear. Repeatedly Joel expressed his repentance and repulsion at his own sinful choices and I believed him, but it was little comfort.

Although home confinement was a gift compared to the alternative of county jail, it came with stiff regulations that required serious adjustments in our lives. Joel was given specific times he could be away from the house; this included certain hours for work daily, a few hours for church on Sunday, and Bible study on Tuesday. On Saturdays he was to be home for the entire day. If an appointment required him to leave the house during those hours, he had to call and get permission a week prior to the appointment. He also had to check in weekly with an officer assigned to his case. This officer came out to the house occasionally to check up on Joel and make sure he was following the home confinement rules. Joel was no longer free to attend a family birthday party, travel to visit his brother a few hours north, or take me on a date night without special permission. He could not even run to the store on a Saturday if he lacked supplies for finishing a home improvement project!

Any time Joel did leave our property, he was required to carry with him a GPS box that monitored his location. If the box started beeping, it meant that his location was lost. In this case he had a few minutes to move, adjust the box, or go outside to get the signal back before the officer assigned to his case would call and ask where he was.

All of these stipulations made us both extremely nervous and served as a regular reminder of the court's perception of Joel. We knew the public mind on these kinds of issues was to assume guilt.

We knew Joel was guilty, but not of everything the court had accused him of. He was not involved in sex tourism in Venezuela; nor had he been involved in distribution of illegal files. We also knew the public would imagine him to be a pedophile, a threat to children, which was certainly not the case.

We knew he would probably have to enter into a plea agreement, but we both still hoped it would be one that kept him from prison or at least would be a short sentence. Some days I imagined we could avoid the whole issue of incarceration. On others I feared a long separation.

As we waited and feared, both of us longed for relief, escape, some way to assuage the pain we lived with daily. It is a natural human response to avoid pain and to do everything we can to satiate it when it cannot be avoided. But when our primary goal is dealing with the pain, we often miss what God has for us in the midst of the pain.

I found that if I could just surround myself with people and work, day in and day out, I could ignore the pain. There were days when I felt like I deserved relief from my pain, and therefore, I allowed myself to indulge in some "harmless" antidote, like a shopping spree or extra chocolate. And there were times when I felt justified in my own "little" sins of frustration and fear, because my life was such a mess. Who wouldn't react impetuously at times?

One night, I was having a real pity party for myself. Joel was working on some project in the backyard, and the kids were waiting for him to spend some time with them. I too had been hoping for a family evening, so even though I appreciated his attempt to get some things done around the house, it was starting to frustrate me that he had picked this evening to do it. After repeated requests that he finish what he was doing and come in, I huffed off to the house to take care of the kids myself and put them into bed. I mumbled to myself about how rude Joel was being and how insensitive he was to the family! I reminded myself of what a good and patient wife I was, and so under-appreciated! Then like a bolt of lightning, God spoke to me, using the words of a dear friend from a recent conversation: "You don't have the 'luxury' of sin, even for one moment." And it hit me like a brick between my eyes that I was the one wasting the time we had left together. I was wasting the opportunity to lean into Christ and to be a helper to my husband. In this case, I had become my own god. Comforting myself and seeing my own needs met with a little family time had become my highest priority.

God's stern correction opened my eyes to the damage I was doing by worshiping self instead of Him. With a humbled and repentant heart, I went back outside to find Joel. Even though he did not need my help on the project he was working on, I stayed outside with him and read aloud to him from a book we had been going through together. Because of God's timely rebuke, at least part of the evening was salvaged as we spent time together, just as I had so longed for. So many times we rob ourselves and others of deep, abiding joy because we are so caught up in the trap of selfishness.

When we refuse to allow the pain to ravage us or when we soothe it with "fixes," we deny ourselves the chance to really discover our core longing, our deepest need and desire for God Himself. In the midst of excruciating circumstances, we seek lesser goals to solve our problem or at least get past the grief of it. Our lesser desires lead us to addiction. Idolatry becomes our modus operandi.

We are all addicted to sin. Every one of us, at times, will succumb to its power in our lives. Addiction haunts the entire human race. The only antidote for the vicious control of sin is the truth of the Gospel spread in our hearts, awakening us to our desire for God.

If our desire for anything is deeper than our longing for God, we begin to feel entitled. We start to see God as a cosmic vending machine. We begin to claim His promises and make demands according to our own agenda and need. And slowly we begin to provide for our own needs when God is not "good enough" or "loving enough" to do it for us. Whatever makes us feel better becomes our addiction. But the feeling never lasts, and we become caught in the vicious cycle.

But when we allow our pain to propel us toward God, then our desire for God is not a demand for His response; it is the worship of brokenness. Often God does not reveal Himself in the way we long for. Often, the tears flow with even more longing. That is why so many are tempted to take care of themselves instead of admitting impotence. But utter helplessness is the doorway through which we must step to truly know God. And often the passageway through which we travel is long and dark and lonely. God does not always, or even often, meet us and comfort us in our pain in the immediate way we expect.

At times our desire for God is met with apparent unresponsiveness from God. Our expectations of a real encounter with Him do not transpire. And our longing intensifies. The psalmist knew this to be true. In chapter 42, he cried out, "As a deer longs for streams of water, so I long for you, O God. I thirst for God, the living God...Day and night I have only tears for food..." (verses 1-3, NLT). He felt the frustration of longing for God as the only water that could satiate his soul and yet not finding Him. Again in Psalms 63:1b, he says, "My soul thirsts for You;

My body longs for You. In a dry and parched land, where there is no water" (NIV).

God is not hiding. He is allowing our desire for Him to grow and to blossom into an all-consuming passion. Our desire for God is a Spirit-driven passion. God is the one driving that desire; therefore, He cannot be absent in our longing. He will fulfill it in His way and His time.

During this new era of waiting, God began to speak into my pain. I longed for relief. My journal filled with cries to God for His interference on our behalf. But I also longed for His joy. I was beginning to understand that joy in the Lord and deep, ragged emotional pain are not mutually exclusive. Rather, our capacity to know Him and rejoice in Him alone is amplified by pain. Psalms 84:6 speaks of those who find their strength in the Lord: "When they walk through the Valley of Weeping, it will become place of refreshing springs." When we allow God to work in our pain, we find that we can live in joy in the middle of unthinkable circumstances.

Before I knew the kind of pain that is now a part of my daily life, I loved God. I desired to know Him better, and I longed to serve Him. What I did not know was how much I needed Him. Now, through inexplicable pain, I have come to recognize that neediness, and it has increased my capacity for knowing and loving Him.

HE IS ALWAYS ENOUGH

Dignity or Brokenness

Shortly after Joel's arrest, I watched the movie, A Mighty Heart, which is based on the true story of the abduction and murder of Daniel Pearl, a journalist who was pursuing a story in Pakistan. The movie was about his wife's response to this horrifying event. She was pregnant with their first child when her husband suddenly disappeared. At first no one knew if he had been kidnapped, and then when that was confirmed, there was great concern about negotiating a release. Everything his wife hoped for was stripped away when the terrorists who had abducted her husband sent a video of his brutal murder at their hands. The movie highlighted how these events had helped her to become a stronger and more compassionate and dignified person through the process of suffering.

As I watched that movie, I identified with her pain and the way she chose to handle it. She rarely cried in front of other people; she remained calm and handled even the most disastrous moments with dignity. I could see myself in her reactions.

At the end of the movie, she offered a moving monologue about how she did not hold a grudge against the people of Pakistan, and how she had learned to be a stronger person through the tragedy.

I was left with the question: "She and I look so much alike in a tragedy, and yet she did not have God. She was not a believer. Can human nature actually grow through pain and achieve a new kind of beauty in the process?" Ultimately I asked God, genuinely and without guile, "What difference do you really make? If, without you, she became a stronger person, what difference do you really make?"

"That woman became stronger through her pain. She grew more independent and self-sufficient through the agony," God told me. "If that is what you're looking for, then you can do that on your own. I've put free will in the heart of every human being. You can exercise that freedom in developing your own independence. But if that's not enough for you, then I AM."

I was stunned to see the contrast. Suddenly it seemed so obvious. God was working toward brokenness, and if I was working toward dignity and personal strength, then He and I were not striving for the same end.

On the outside, both ends might look similar. God desires to fill me with the grace to live in the joy of His presence in spite of present circumstances. At a passing glance, this might look like dignity and strength, but a closer assessment will reveal that it is really brokenness. In contrast to dignity and strength, living a life of brokenness means constant reliance on a strength outside of myself. It is characterized by an unceasing awareness of my own frailty and subsequent need for God.

Brokenness is something we shy away from in our cultured society. It is hard to see brokenness as a good thing. No one wants to admit helplessness.

In contrast, independence is seen as a virtue. Doing things differently from others and standing out in the crowd is admired. Americans like to think of themselves as creators of their own destinies. It is a trait to be proud of. After all, didn't we start the independence movement? Our entire system is based on autonomy. Individualism is a heralded part of our society's culture.

The women's movement is a perfect cultural example of the pride we take in independence. Women over the years have banded together to prove that they can take on the world. They have argued that they are capable of doing the same jobs men do with equal if not enhanced success. They compete in the political world, the athletic world, and especially the business world. Women today disdain the idea of being dependent on a man for provision.

This societal standard has become such a norm that Christian women very easily buy into its deception. The idea of needing someone else, especially a man, has become scorned and even repulsive. "We are capable, we are intelligent, we are determined. Therefore, we can take care of ourselves," today's modern woman says.

As God worked in my heart, I began to see this pursuit of independence as a fleshly pursuit, a total misuse of the gift of free will that God has given me. And I began to see the emptiness in that pursuit. I realized that I do not want to be like that woman in the movie. I do not want to end up stronger and more self-possessed as a result of this tragedy. If that is all I am going to learn, then it is not worth the pain! Thus my prayer became, "Oh, Lord, to whom shall I go? I have believed, and I know that you are the Christ, the Holy one of God!" (John 6:68, paraphrased).

This realization was only the beginning, however, in yielding my prideful, independent heart to God. The writer of Psalms 119 states, "I will walk at liberty because I keep your commandments" (vs. 45). That seems like a totally contradictory statement if we do not understand what true freedom is. True freedom is living a life of total surrender to my sovereign Lord and Creator. When I am living in surrender to Him, I am free: free from worry, free from self-imposed rules, free from selfish desires, free from sin, and free from others' expectations. It is tremendously refreshing to live in that kind of liberty.

Each time I began to panic about my situation, God would whisper to my heart, "Am I really enough for you?" and I would cry back, "Oh, yes, Lord! You are enough! I have believed, and I know that you are the Christ."

Empty Hands

Many days, God did not feel very close. I did not know if I was hanging onto Him out of sheer desperation or if what I had always believed would actually prove to be true. But I knew I had nowhere else to go. Complete surrender was my only recourse.

Strangely, even that seemed to bring me a glimmer of self-satisfaction. I was doing the right thing, holding my empty hands up to God and begging for His goodness to be poured into my life. But often God did not hop to it and meet me in my helplessness nor rescue me from our plight as I expected. I did not yet understand that even when we beg God for good things, He can remain silent and unresponsive. We know we have nothing to offer God, yet we offer Him our helplessness, holding it up like a trophy to be admired and expectantly awaiting heavenly applause and then some prompt aid. As long as we expect to elicit a response from God in this manner, we will not truly understand or experience friendship with God. It was a long journey, but God's resistance to my manipulation was really a response of love. It was what I needed to drive the pride from my heart and render me truly desirous of Him and Him alone.

Slowly it dawned on me in the midst of my pain that while I longed for rescue and relief, I wanted God more. I began to pray with Habakkuk, "Though the fig tree may not blossom nor fruit be in the vines; though the labor of the olive tree may fail and the fields yield no food...yet I will rejoice in the Lord, I will joy in the God of my salvation" (3:17a, 18, NKJV) God was indeed giving me the grace to live in His joy in the middle of our unthinkable circumstances.

The Beauty of Brokenness

Joel and I started to read the book *Don't Waste Your Life* by John Piper during the spring while we were awaiting his trial date. Piper's assertion in this book is that glorifying God and enjoying Him forever are not two exclusive ends of man but were rather the same end expressed in two different ways. Joel and I both found this compelling. Our reading was punctuated with discussion as we began to internalize the idea of enjoying God as a chief means of glorifying Him.

We were both eager to enjoy God, in spite of our circumstances. But what we were learning was that we could enjoy God because of our circumstances, and in doing so, we would bring Him great glory. Praise that comes from absolute desolation speaks to the world of a sovereign, loving God.

This again brings to mind Job's story. Satan did not really think Job's worship of God was authentic because it came from a place of security and prosperity. Many individuals will contend similarly that Christians are only happy when God is blessing them. When we can express our complete rest in Him in the middle of excruciating and sometimes unfair circumstances, we have the opportunity to show the world that no matter what the situation, He is enough.

We had been thrown into a situation that demanded just that kind of response. If we were to glorify God and enjoy Him, we were going to do it in the middle of the painful scenario in which we were living. It could not be separate from our circumstances, for they were the baseline that showed God to be so totally sufficient.

One day as I was pondering Habakkuk 3:17, it struck me that the writer did not say, "Until the fig tree blossoms...I will rejoice in you." He said, "Although the fig tree doesn't blossom...I will rejoice in you." The joy we find in God is not contingent on things getting better. So although Joel and I both hoped for a merciful solution to our situation, one that would not require a long separation, we were finding that no matter what happened, we could enjoy God and thereby glorify Him.

More than Conquerors

Romans 8 speaks of God's incredible love for us. Paul contends that nothing can separate us from that love. If anyone had a platform for expressing this, it would be Paul. He had experienced so much adversity and tragedy in his years of serving Christ. Humanly speaking, it would have been understandable for him to become disillusioned with God and even question God's involvement or care. But instead, Paul wrote extremely convincing arguments about the absolute power of God's love from which we can never be separated.

Then Paul finished with this dramatic promise, "In all these things, we are more than conquerors." Piper suggests that to be more than conquerors is to subjugate the enemy and use him for God's purposes.[viii] In our case, Joel and I begged God to subjugate Joel's sin and to use the consequences of that sin to bring about a wealth of good for His glory. Satan may have meant to destroy Joel and indeed our entire family through the sinful choices Joel made. But because we are more than conquerors "through Him who loved us," God would turn it around and use this whole tragedy to work His good purpose.

The Verdict Is In

There were many setbacks during the period between Joel's arrest and his sentencing hearing. We had complicated meetings and phone calls with the attorney as a plea agreement was discussed.

I cherished each day we had together but felt a constant awareness of the impending future.

Finally, the sentencing hearing was set for May 22, the boys' first day of summer vacation. I found myself anticipating that day with a mixture of dread and resignation. Part of me was just longing to get it over with. At the same time, I knew whatever happened on May 22 would really be marking a new beginning for us, maybe a formidable beginning of many months or even years apart.

On May 5, almost three weeks before the looming date of the hearing, I wrote these words in my journal:

> My heart feels like it's bleeding out, and tears come randomly. I find myself in this abyss of agony with a panicked notion that I may sink even further. Ezra 7:28b says, "I felt encouraged because the gracious hand of the Lord my God was on me." Oh, God, please put your gracious hand on me!

Each day carried its own dread, and I was not used to recoiling from the future. It felt like a strange about-face from the anticipation I had felt while waiting for our wedding. Such a joy that countdown had held. This on the other hand was like watching a car accident in slow motion: one long, drawn-out, panic-stricken wait for the inevitable. I wondered what it must be like for cancer patients who have been told they have only a few weeks or months left to live. It would have been easy to let the dread consume us, and on some days, it did. But overall we by God's grace made the most of the time we had together and purposed to let Him hold the future.

We spent our last day together, trying to cram in as much time with family as possible. Joel took the boys out to a movie and to dinner at their favorite pizza place. I wanted to join them because being away from Joel was so painful, but I also knew they needed this time with their dad. So I found my way over to my older sister's and wiled away the time with her.

Tammy is intuitive with a strong, abiding sense of justice. She is precise about everything she does, and she maintains an unusually high standard for herself and those around her. She is also loving, patient, constantly aware of God's hand in things, though not unwilling or incapable of offering her case up before Him, and perhaps most importantly, unfailingly loyal. I, on the other hand, have been known to be excessively hasty. I am energetic, impulsive, and fun-loving. I am strong-willed and do not mind standing out in a crowd. She and I have always been the most unlikely best friends. However, our friendship has grown from the time we were little girls, and she was the person I knew I could rely on to be with me in the pain I was experiencing on that last day before the inevitable hearing. She would not try to fix my pain or even ease it. She would just be with me.

After their time out, Joel and the boys returned, and we regrouped at our house with other family surrounding us with their love and support. When everyone had gone home, Joel and I spent the remainder of the evening and ensuing night sharing in our grief, discussing what we were saying good-bye to and what we hoped God would do. We ended the night by praying together before fitful sleep mercifully enveloped us both.

Although much grief surrounded May 22, God's loving care through His precious people is what I will always remember as I look back. The courtroom was full of family and friends. My dad sat at my right and my sister, Tammy, to my left, holding my hand.

When I was asked to testify, I felt as if God just poured His words right through me. I declared my love and forgiveness of Joel, comparing it to that of Christ for us, though in such small measure. In that moment, I knew the love of my Savior like I had never known it before. I felt a deep, abiding love for Joel as a result.

Before the judge handed down his sentence, he looked out at his full courtroom and commented, "I do not know if I have ever seen my courtroom this full, especially not in a case like this." Then he looked at Joel and said, "You are a truly blessed man to have these kinds of friends." It was clear how remarkable he found the support and love with which we were surrounded.

As we left the courtroom—Joel having been sentenced to an eternity of sixty-three months and led away under armed guard—I could feel God's glory in that place. He had been honored and would be honored in our lives, in spite of our sin and its consequences, and in spite of and indeed through the pain of our separation. Romans 8:28 was being fulfilled in and through our own lives.

Nevertheless, I felt as if I had just been tossed into a whirlpool and was being swept away as Joel attempted to call me from county jail that first evening with limited success. For one reason or another, we could not seem to connect, and I knew I could not return his calls. I kept hoping he would try again, and I was fearing that he would not. I knew he was equally desperate to talk to me, but I had no idea how the phone system would work in the county jail and how long he would have to keep trying. A feeling of desperation and helplessness engulfed me. My new reality threatened to overwhelm me.

If God had not been so faithfully working in my life with His precious assurances, I do not know how I would have survived that first day. I was reassured and comforted by the prayers and support of our family and friends.

But in some ways this only added to my agony as I kept thinking of Joel alone in an unfamiliar setting, with no one to comfort him. I was nearly frantic as I attempted to process what his new reality must be like.

Facing the Music

Going back to our house and packing up Joel's clothes and other belongings haunted me. I did not want to leave his stuff out lying around, but I did not want to put it away either. Both options were abhorrent, one for the constant reminder that he was gone, and the other for the finality of knowing he was gone. Fresh waves of agony undulated through our home as I sorted his belongings, choosing what should be packed away and kept, and what should be donated to some charity. My sister and mom lovingly joined me in the agonizing task. With methodical detachment I managed to sort his belongings. I was thankful to have something from Daddy's stuff to give to each of the older boys, a small reminder of their dad even when he was far away. In the end, the task was done, and even though I felt an acute emptiness around the house, I knew it was the only practical step to take given the length of his sentence.

Neither of us had anticipated how rough county jail would be. Fighting was common, and Joel spent most of his time in protective custody because of threats against him. Inmates have their own criteria for rating crimes, and since they assumed Joel had done more than store illegal images, he was the low man on the totem pole as far as most were concerned. Joel, who already felt a deep sense of disgust and self-reproach, felt intensely their rejection and harassment.

Protective custody also meant little to no time in the yard; he was locked up in his cell twenty-four hours a day, with limited access to a phone for calls to me. He was not even allowed regular showers since that meant leaving his cell and required guard escorts. His frustration and helplessness escalated through instances like repeatedly asking for a pencil to write me and waiting for days on end until a guard finally decided to get him one. Simple things like not having a watch or a clock to look at added to the mind game he was playing. Half the time, he didn't know if it was morning or evening. There was no system or standard. Joel was simply at the mercy of the guards' whims.

Joel was indeed learning through the incredible academy of loss that Jesus is enough. When everything was stripped away and he found himself helplessly waiting on an uncaring prison guard for even his most basic needs, he found that God is enough. Joel wrote in one of his letters, "I still struggle daily with trusting Him with the details of what I perceive to be my needs, but I keep coming back to the fact that He is my greatest need."[ix]

Often, as I lay at night, painfully aware of the emptiness of our king-size bed, I would beg God to feel His presence and to know His closeness in a new way that would allay the hurt and let me sleep. And many nights what kept me from sleeping was my concern for Joel and his safety. There were so many unknowns for him and so much that I could not find out in our short phone conversations and visits every few days.

I remember being turned away one day in particular when I went to visit Joel. I was told he had been moved into protective custody. Joel had not called me or told me of any move. But he had shared with me just the morning before that he was concerned for his safety after seeing a story in the paper about his crime. Since I had not had a phone call for a couple days and they would not explain to me what the move meant, I began to fear the worst. Desperate to hear from Joel, I tried calling our lawyer and later the chaplain of the jail. After what seemed like an eternity of waiting and several phone calls, I was informed that Joel was fine but had been moved for his own safety, and the phone in the area where he was moved was out of order, so he could not make calls. Although I was relieved, I was still desperate to see Joel and talk to him, to know that he really was okay. These kinds of issues tore at my heart. My helplessness constantly threw me into the arms of my Savior.

I also found myself in the frustrating situation of waiting in line to get a visiting slot and often finding out that his visiting hours had changed, and I would have to try again another day. Visiting was a challenge, but we both were so desperate to see one another that I worked very hard at following the system and getting there every time he was allowed to have visits.

One afternoon as I was expressing these burdens to my younger sister, Dar Gail, she wisely commented, "I perceive that you are having an easier time trusting God with yourself than you are with Joel."

"Of course," I replied, "because I know what is going on with us, and we are in a predictable environment." But even as I answered her, I felt the conviction of the Holy Spirit. Did I really trust God at all? If I could only trust Him with known circumstances, what kind of trust was that? I had to relinquish control and my desire to fix things and allow God to be enough, not only for me, but also for my precious, suffering husband.

One of the most painful parts of those visits was the glass between us. We could see each other and hear each other, but not touch or feel each other. We could not hold back the tears as Roman, then barely one, would bang on the glass and yell, "Dada!"

It was one thing to believe Jesus was enough for me. It was quite another to come to the realization that He is enough for each one of us, whether we are together or apart in this crisis. Joel's deepest needs would be met by God Himself, even in a lonely prison cell. My children would find comfort in Him. When I could not be both mommy and daddy to them, He would be enough. God supplies our greatest need with Himself.

MY SERVICE, HIS GIFT

Time Off

One of my most immediate physical concerns after Joel's sentencing was providing for my family. Joel and I had always felt that it was of paramount importance that I be in the home for our children, so we had never been a two-income household. Furthermore, as missionaries, our work had been together. I had taught at the mission school in Venezuela, but only part-time, and I arranged my own schedule to fit that of my children and husband. It was somewhat of a tag-team operation. Now I was faced with the need to become primary breadwinner for our family. I did not want to work full-time and leave my kids for someone else, even family, to look after. But I was left with little choice. I also still felt very burdened to continue in ministry, but that seemed unlikely. How could one person do all that two people had been busy doing?

Joel was incarcerated the end of May, and our counselor suggested that I not work for the summer to give our family time to adjust to all the changes we were facing. I liked this idea but knew it did not seem very practical since I had no savings to live on. However, my family encouraged me to accept their help with finances and to trust God for direction in getting a job in the fall.

So even though it seemed like a risky move, I agreed to pray about work and take the summer off to be with my kids. What a blessing from the Lord to have that time to concentrate on adjusting to our new life. We spent many hours trying to visit Joel, first in county jail and later when he was moved much farther away. It would have been very hard to be as supportive of Joel and available to him if I had been tied down by a job.

Some Dreams Are Made of Reality

As a little girl growing up in a remote jungle location, my education needs were met through a small mission-operated school that always seemed to be short-staffed. After all, what educated individual wants to give up modern life to settle in a remote location and teach children at a school with few to no amenities or bonuses?

Our classrooms were designed to function with two grade levels in the same room. And even then, the size of the entire class rarely rose above ten. The whole school from first to twelfth grade consisted of no more than fifty-five students. So while we felt the need for qualified teachers acutely, there was no great outcry to fill that need. It was, understandably, a thankless job.

When I was in fourth grade, I had a wonderfully creative teacher, Mr. Moore, who was especially adept at building in us a love of history and a pride for our own mother country. He treated our class as though we were bright enough and qualified enough to go out into the world and make a difference. He never acted as though he had condescended to teach us, but rather, he acted as though it was his greatest calling. His influence built in me a desire to teach. From that point on, I determined that I would make a difference in the lives of MK's. I would get my education, and I would come back to the jungle in order to serve God by teaching history to kids at a mission school.

This dream was short-lived, however. Our time in Venezuela at the MK school was cut short because of the political unrest in that country. And when Joel was charged and sent to prison, I imagined my years of teaching in Venezuela to be the only chance I would ever have to minister to MK's. After all, what mission board would be interested in employing me, knowing my family's predicament? Nevertheless, I imagined teaching at the small Christian school that is a part of New Tribes Mission's headquarters right here in central Florida. This seemed impossible, having been required to resign from the mission along with my husband.

I was thankful for my education and began to wonder what kind of paying job I could get in order to provide for my family. It was a daunting idea. I found myself in another one of those valleys where only God knew the way out. I wasn't even sure how to go about searching for a job in the public teaching arena. Furthermore, my heart still longed to be in full-time ministry.

God had not taken away my desire to participate in the furtherance of the Gospel through full-time work. But I didn't see how that desire could be fulfilled.

Then one day, my sister who works for Wycliffe Associates, a mission organization based in Orlando,

Florida, came to me and asked what I would think of joining their team. They have no requirement that both spouses be members. They treat each missionary as an individual employee. What's more, they lend their missionaries to other mission boards on a short- or long-term basis, related to the specific needs involved. After some research, I found that New Tribes Mission would indeed be happy to have me on board as a teacher at their school, seconded to them through Wycliffe Associates. The only catch: I would have to raise my own support. And I would receive no paychecks until I reached 100 percent of their required support for my specific ministry. This seemed crazy! But I knew if God wanted me serving Him in a professional position, He would raise up individuals to join with me financially.

Financial partnership is a huge job though, and I had just one summer to raise everything I needed if I was going to start working in the fall. To complicate matters further, I didn't have the finances or capacity to begin a long speaking or traveling tour to raise funds. I was functioning as a single parent, trying to adjust to a completely new set of circumstances with my husband in prison. Some of our supporters from previous years on the field might be a good place to start. But others were so far removed from our lives that they didn't even know what had happened to our family. It seemed an impossible task.

Good Gifts from a Loving God

Jesus told His disciples in Matthew 7:11, "If you sinful people know how to give good gifts to your children, how much more will your heavenly Father give good gifts to those who ask Him" (NLT). Prior to this, Jesus was talking about praying effectively, persistently, and with genuine faith. This passage has often been misused to say that anything we sincerely ask God for, believing He will do it, will be ours. Experience, along with the body of contending Scripture, should indeed clarify that Jesus certainly did not mean such a thing! God is not some cosmic vending machine full of good treats that He passes out when we put in the right change—faith and persistence.

One thing we must again remember is that God defines "good" on His own terms, not on ours. Jesus does not say God will give us whatever we want. He says God will give us good gifts. Those good gifts will be according to His sovereign will as we prayerfully surrender to Him. Through prayer we acknowledge our neediness and dependence on God. When we pray in faith, truly believing that God is in control and that He is eternally good, then we can accept His gifts as good.

Jesus was very clearly assuring His disciples that no matter what evidence they might experience to the contrary, God is good, and His intentions toward His children are always good. When our heart's desire is aligned with Christ, we know that what God gives us is good.

The Desire and the Power to Please Him

In Philippians 2:14, Paul states, "It is God who is working in you giving you the desire and power to do what pleases Him" (NLT). His good gift to us then is the desire and power to obey Him and do the things that will please Him. I knew if God wanted me to continue in ministry, He would provide for that. He had certainly given me the desire. Now I needed the means or the power to follow through.

In one giant leap of faith, I sent out letters to as many people as I could think of who knew our situation and who might be interested in partnering with me financially. I say this was a giant leap of faith, because I have to admit that my pride was getting in the way at this point and kept accusing me of becoming a beggar. I even remember saying to someone, "I don't want people to support me financially out of pity." While that may sound justifiable on the surface, it clearly had me at the center. My focus was inward. God has proved Himself entirely capable of taking resources and using them for His glory, no matter what their original intent.

When the disciples asked Jesus what should be done about the crowds that were gathered to hear him preach, because the hour was late and they needed food, none of them expected him to suggest that they should feed the crowd. But that is exactly what Jesus did. Obviously, they had no resources to feed the crowd. However, that did not bother Jesus. He gave them a few simple instructions, and as they obeyed, He provided in abundance. This is the way my financial partnership base with Wycliffe Associates was built. He asked me to take small steps of faith that demonstrated I was listening to Him and not to my pride. Then He provided in abundance. Within six weeks, I was receiving 100 percent of the needed funds. It appeared almost unnoticeably in so many ways that I honestly to this day do not know how it happened. I am sure the disciples who watched Jesus bless the bread and fish that day thought the same thing. It just happened!

God had given me the resources needed to do what pleased Him. With an overwhelmed heart, I began working at the mission school in Sanford, Florida, just a few miles from my home. It was the same school my kids were attending, which was an added blessing. I found myself again in the privileged position of ministering to missionaries by teaching their children.

Many of the students at the school are there on a short-term basis as their parents transition from the United States to overseas, or from one foreign assignment to another. Others are in the United States because of an illness or other family emergency. Still others are children whose parents work full-time in the ministry of keeping nearly 3000 missionaries functioning effectively overseas. I find it an exciting challenge to interact with these kids and share with them as they experience the many ups and downs that are typical of MK life.

My Service Is God's Gift to Me

Going to work outside the home was a daunting task for me. Even though I had been a missionary teacher in Venezuela, my schedule was part-time. Furthermore, I did not feel the responsibility of breadwinner for the family. Once that was laid squarely on my shoulders, I wondered how I would handle the schedule. What would it be like to work all day and come home to all the work still waiting for me? The truth is, it is not easy. Most days it is exhausting. But one thing that keeps me from discouragement in my exhaustion is thankfulness. When I find myself bone weary, God reminds me of what a precious gift it is to find myself "weary in well-doing." If I'm going to be worn out, I want it to be in keeping with building God's kingdom.

Recently I was listening to a message by Pete Briscoe on one of my jogs in the neighborhood. I love how he made this point, saying, "Your service or ministry is God's gift to you, not your gift to Him."ˣ God chooses to use us. He doesn't have to. Several examples in Scripture remind us that He is entirely capable of accomplishing His purpose by employing other parts of His creation.

Jonah sticks out as just such an example. The Bible tells us that God had prepared a great fish to swallow Jonah. Then God instructed the fish to spit Jonah out. Apparently the fish was more cooperative than Jonah, much to Jonah's benefit! So why does God continue to use humans when our free will often gets in the way? God delights to use us and to expose His glory to the world! He has created us for just such a purpose. It is His plan that we enjoy making much of Him.

Having this focus relieves me of so much stress. Serving in His kingdom is a gift from God. Being a part of MKs' lives at a little school in central Florida is one way to make much of my Savior. And as I wearily climb into bed, mentally checking off one more day, I thank God for continuing to give me the desire and the power to do what pleases Him.

THE POWER OF FRIENDSHIP

A Simple Act of Kindness

It was a Friday, so I had finished school early and was home by lunchtime. I was walking up the steps when I noticed something propped up against the door. It was a vase with roses and a note! The note was a simple Valentine's Day card with "Love, Joel" written inside. I could not imagine how Joel had managed this little gift since he was barricaded behind razor wire in a federal facility nearly three hours away. This was my first Valentine's Day alone. I knew he had to have had help, but I could not think of whom. My in-laws were out of town, so I knew right away it could not have been them. I called my mom, hoping to catch a clue from her tone of voice. (She's not a great secret keeper.) But she seemed genuinely surprised and assured me she had nothing to do with it. None of my other family members seemed to know where the flowers had come from either. I was overwhelmed by the thoughtfulness of some unknown friend who never was revealed. My first Valentine's Day became a day to celebrate God's precious kindness to me, even in the absence of my beloved.

Our Reticence to Share in One Another's Suffering

Before I faced the tragedy I am now living in from day to day, I often felt awkward comforting someone who was truly grieving. I wanted to enter into their pain and grieve with them, but I did not know how. It seems like a fairly common struggle. Rejoicing with those that rejoice is often so much easier than weeping with those that weep.

When we hear stories of others who have suffered greatly, our hearts recoil in fear of experiencing such suffering ourselves. Our efforts to help them feel better are partially selfish. We want the assurance that there is a "feel better" place, because we are terrified of experiencing the same loss and not finding relief.

Reaching out to someone in grief is also difficult because instinctively we feel that we have so little to offer. I know I have felt helpless to offer people the kind of comfort they need. I look at their suffering and think, Nothing I could say will even matter considering what they are going through. Unfortunately, this lack of confidence in our own ability to help keeps us from trying.

One final barrier to comforting others is that in our modern culture, there is very little room given for grieving. Many tribal cultures have long periods set aside for people to grieve the loss of a loved one. They also have established cultural symbols that allow others who might not otherwise know to see that the person is in mourning. In American culture, we do not have these patterns. Often people who are experiencing a long and agonizing trial are expected to buck up and put on a stoic front. It is hard to reach out and help someone who does not look like they need help.

Again, I think of the story of Joseph, who suffered greatly but obviously learned to totally rely on God. It is obvious that he missed his father and brother, Benjamin, very much during the years of separation. There is no indication that Joseph squelched his feelings, denying his emotions, and presenting a stoic front. As a matter of fact, the Bible records that when he revealed himself to his brothers, he wept loudly, so loudly, in fact, that his servants worried that something was wrong. Joseph did not deny the pain he experienced. Scripture also tells us that when he heard that his brothers feared he would take revenge once their father died, he broke down crying. He was devastated that they were afraid of him after he had shown them so much kindness.

Joseph was not a stoic. But he allowed God to rule in his life above and beyond his emotions; and out of the agony of unbelievable treachery, God brought him to a place of redemption and wholeness, a place of honor, and opportunity for service.

There is a tendency when in the midst of incredible pain to sanitize our emotions and handle our pain. But this is really a barrier to the true joy that lies down the long path of suffering. We never get there because we create our own little world of "okay reality" to avoid the crushing pain. We anesthetize ourselves against the deepest pain, pretending it away and expecting that eventually, it will fade from reality.

I was tremendously comforted to know it is okay to feel deeply the emotional anguish accompanied by loss. On top of our already somewhat stoic American culture, popular Christian culture often implies that prolonged grief indicates a lack of trust in God. The Christian community as a whole does not know how to handle the suffering of prolonged tragedy. It is expected that grieving will not last and that in the grieving, there will be an overriding emphasis on God's care. This, of course, means one should not question God openly or share grief in a hopeless manner. Testimonies of pain should always include a hopeful outlook and an emphasis on faith in God's ultimate good purpose. To expose our real pain makes us look ungodly.

Because many Christians feel obligated to abide by these unwritten rules, they hide their true emotions and put on a godly front. It is rare to find someone who lives out honestly the pain they experience. And it is a struggle to know how to help someone grieve who is totally aware of God's power and love, and still feels utterly desolate in their pain.

This idea that God expects us to rise above our pain and live in total acceptance of Him without experiencing emotional anguish leads to a very destructive form of Christian Buddhism. The idea is that if we can only desire God enough, the other things in life will not matter and therefore cannot hurt us. Of course, desiring God above all else is quintessential to a dynamic relationship with Him. But God wants us to truly desire Him for the sake of knowing Him, not simply to avoid pain on this earth. Furthermore, no matter how much we desire God above all else, we may find ourselves in excruciating emotional agony. Desiring God and knowing that He has our best interest at heart may give us a gracious peace to endure, but it does not eliminate the sadness. Contrary to modern Christian theology, we can be totally at peace with God and still grieve deeply. Sorrow and joy can dance together and often do.

Larry Crabb in his book, *Shattered Dreams,* suggests that this commonly accepted but erroneous idea about suffering causes people who are grieving to retreat into themselves, hiding their pain and wearing a public mask of peace and dignity, trying to look strong. God's call to brokenness is thereby thwarted, and the intended function of the body of Christ is impaired.[xi] It is hard to minister God's grace and compassion to people who pretend to be strong enough not to need it. Joel and I had both practiced this kind of "Christian Buddhism" when we had returned from Venezuela. And Joel now admits that his refusal to seek comfort and help in a time of neediness only fueled his addiction to lesser comforts.

What God Says About Grieving and Trusting

Scripture has very different ideas about pain and suffering that are completely contrary to popular Christian culture. If trusting God and experiencing deep emotional pain are mutually exclusive, then Jesus Himself did not trust God, which, of course, is complete blasphemy. Christ wept over the poor choices of Jerusalem and the Jewish nation.

He wept at the grief He saw in His friends at the graveside of Lazarus. He wept in the garden at the pending doom He was about to face alone. Jesus showed incredibly strong emotions, and He never quit trusting God. He was so distressed in the garden that He sweated "great drops of blood." Clearly as the sinless Son of God, He could not be accused of not trusting God enough. Even when we trust God, the pain can be excruciating.

Another example is Martha when her brother, Lazarus, died. She rushed out of the house to meet Jesus when she heard He was coming. Her words to him are painful and precious: "Oh, Lord, if You had been here, my brother would not have died. But I know, even now, God will give You whatever You ask." Martha expressed deep faith in her Savior, while still feeling a cavernous loss. She knew Jesus could have changed things. She might have even thought He should have. Her pain was raw, and she may have felt a little ripped off that Jesus had not been around to fix things when they could still be fixed. But even in her grief, she trusted Him.

Psalms is filled with verses that describe the anguish of a hurting soul. God clearly does not expect us to aspire to emotionless trust in Him. On the contrary, the Bible assures us that "the Lord is close to the brokenhearted" (Psalms 34:18a, NIV).

God gave Isaiah this message for Hezekiah regarding his earlier prophecy that the king would die. "Go tell Hezekiah...I have heard your prayers and seen your tears. I will add fifteen more years to your life" (Isaiah 38:5, NIV). God gave Hezekiah fifteen more years of life! He saw Hezekiah's grief, and it meant something to Him.

As I struggled with the "proper way to grieve" and what God's Word says about our emotional response to pain, I was struck by Daniel's reaction to his vision of God's impending judgment. He became physically ill! He was in such dread of the future that he became sick. There are many instances in the Old Testament where God's prophets suffered physically and emotionally as they followed and obeyed God. This is a great comfort to me. I can feel intense emotional pain and even cry out to God in that kind of pain without denying His power.

Sadness is not a sin; it does not indicate a lack of trust or rest in God. What we do know is that we do not have to sorrow without hope! Because we have a confident trust that God is working for our good, even in our sorrow, we will find joy. We will not grieve like "people who have no hope" (1 Thess. 4:13, NLT) .This does not mean we will not feel deeply the pain of loss, as many biblical examples prove.

Not All "Comfort" is Equally Comforting

It is a natural tendency for us to try to help those who are grieving to feel better. Instead of weeping with those that weep, we try to get those that weep to laugh with us. Without meaning to, this trivializes the pain. I remember telling my family once, "When someone sees me being sorrowful and suggests a simple solution like taking me out to coffee, it is like saying to me that a date out for coffee will fix the fact that my husband is in federal prison." This might sound a little caustic, and perhaps in my raw emotional state, I tended toward judgment. It was not the genuine offers for time spent together that I scorned. It was the seemingly flippant offers that were weighted down with the idea that I needed to get over it and get on with life. It seemed excessively simplistic to me to think that some outing would "get my mind off it."

One of the reasons we find it hard to comfort those who mourn is because we think on the surface. We cannot change the situation, so we attempt to affect change in others' responses. We see strong sorrowful emotions as a negative and try to help people overcome those feelings. Denying the emotions of pain and suffering will only develop calloused hearts. Allowing that pain to run its course creates new channels of compassion and carves out cavernous ravines to be filled with the river of God's love. Just as we do not value waiting, neither do we value pain as we should. Clearly, suffering both physically and emotionally are avenues to increased capacity. To inhibit that in a suffering friend's life is really doing him a disservice.

I also struggled with frustration when people gave me an ambiguous offer for help and never followed up with tangible aid. Well-meaning Christians said things like, "Let me know if there is anything I can do to help." But they never followed up with concrete help. People who are thrown into neediness are not likely to even know how to ask for the specific help they need. So it is a real demonstration of God's love and care when someone volunteers to participate in a specific way.

I have learned a lot about how God uses the body of Christ to minister grace and healing to those who suffer. The friends and family that He has put into our lives have been a testament to His powerful work.

Shortly after Joel's arrest, Karis, one of my dearest childhood friends, called to see how I was doing. We have remained close throughout the years, even though we have not lived near each other for most of our adult lives. She was living 1500 miles away, yet she wanted to know if there was anything she could do. I mentioned to her how much I had enjoyed a Christian music CD she had given me for my birthday the year before. A few days later, I received a package in the mail with three more CD's. She also sent me scores of sermons on CD that were such a blessing and encouragement to me. This dear friend offered to help and then followed through in a tangible way.

I found myself hungering for little reminders of God from moment to moment, and Christian music became a part of that. Another friend of mine who lived locally came over to my house one day and gave me a Christian music CD full of songs she felt spoke to my pain. Her words of encouragement bolstered me as she told me how every time she heard the one song, it was a reminder to pray for me because it was a picture of what God was doing in my life.

Joel and I went through an era in which we felt like lepers. It is hard for Christians to reach out and really know how to be with one another in painful situations. It is even harder when the difficult situation involves shameful sins, even if repentance has occurred. Those who were not afraid to enter into our messy world and identify with us, even in a time of great shame, left indelible marks on our lives.

Toni, a friend from our church who had been Jaden's Sunday school teacher, demonstrated a kind and unassuming form of forgiveness and love. Although she knew we were outcasts as far as the church was concerned, she would randomly drop by our house with gifts. She brought the boys backpacks full of school supplies a few weeks before school started. She dropped off some hand-me-down clothes from one of her older children. She came by one day near Christmas with homemade soup, fresh fruit from her citrus trees, and presents for the boys! Sometimes she would stay for a short visit; sometimes she was just passing by to drop things off. Her kindness has always been offered out of a heart of love, not in a condescending manner. Her gifts and actions have shouted to us of God's love.

Not long after Joel's incarceration, some special friends of ours from our years in Venezuela were traveling through Florida. They contacted me to see if we could get together. I was very blessed and encouraged when they wanted to know how it would work to see Joel. Usually, in order to visit Joel in county jail, one had to be put on a visitor list made up monthly by Joel. Since Joel did not know that this family was going to be in town, he had not put their names on the list. But I checked at the jail to ask if there was any way that an out-of-town friend could come in with me for visit. I was amazed when they gave permission. Joel was visibly moved by the opportunity to see his friend, even though it was under such devastating circumstances. Both he and I were overcome by the genuine love of these friends. Their desire to participate in our suffering was a beautiful demonstration of Christ's love.

Another family, the Kemps, with whom we had been friends for years, called and asked if I would like to get away to their house for a few days of respite and reflection. At first I declined because they lived so far away in Ohio. I did not have the money for a ticket, even if I found a good deal. But they persisted, shopping for a flight online and finally buying me a ticket when they were sure that I would come. So in July I headed up to Ohio for six days of retreat. What refreshment to my soul to have this time away from my regular duties and responsibilities at home and to spend it with good friends who were willing to be with me in whatever state I was in. Their generosity and kindness has left an indelible mark on our lives.

Summer Bounty

My parents and Joel's were very generous and helped to pay my mortgage in June and July. God's provision was evident during this time, as all our physical needs were met by family and friends.

As the summer wound to an end and we headed into August, I wondered what I was going to do for the mortgage payment. I knew I could borrow it from my father-in-law, but I really did not want to. I was not exactly worried about it, since God had graciously provided for every other need during the summer. But I knew the first was fast approaching, and I had no money in the bank to make the payment.

Just a few days before the payment was due, I picked up the mail and found a letter and package from dear family friends in Wisconsin. They had sent me a couple music CD's and a lovely card. As I opened the card, a check fell out. I was stunned to see that it was more than I needed to cover my mortgage! With great rejoicing, I deposited it in the bank in time to make my payment. Their generosity and concern for us again bolstered my faith and reminded me of God's great love for us.

Compassion Multiplied

The genuine compassion of so many friends in our lives has increased our desire and ability to demonstrate compassion. A person who is compassionate does not offer pat answers or give sage advice for situations they have never experienced. A person who is compassionate will be honest and not ignore another's pain. A person who is compassionate will be willing to sit "in sack cloth and ashes" with their grieving friend and say nothing. Those who were not afraid to get dirty by climbing into our messy lives taught us these beautiful principles of compassion and the power of friendship.

LEANING IN TO HIM

When Joel was placed in county jail, we were told it could take up to six weeks for him to be placed in a federal facility and that we would not know when they would take him or where, until he was on his way. This is for security purposes, but not having a criminal mindset, this dearth of information was hard to accept. I knew it was very likely that I would show up and stand in line to get my turn to visit Joel, only to be told that he was no longer there. Fear wrestled for a place in my heart, and it was a constant battle to refuse it entrance.

I also knew that Joel could be placed at any federal facility, even as far away as Texas, so while I prayed for a close location, I struggled with imagining the worst. Joel was desperate to be moved because of the poor conditions at the county jail and the constant threats. Protective custody left him feeling a bit stir crazy.

As we dragged through the fifth week of his incarceration, Joel told me that they usually moved guys in the middle of the night on Tuesdays, so he was hoping to go the following Tuesday. It was just a couple of weeks before his birthday, and I was not sure I was ready to face all the changes that would come with having him in a federal facility. But I could tell he was feeling increasingly eager to move.

On Monday night I had gone to bed and fallen into a deep sleep when I was awakened by a strange premonition. It was as if God was saying to me, "Joel needs your prayers. He is in a vulnerable position and is being moved with other potentially violent criminals." The strangest part of this was that I felt no fear, just a confidence that God was in control, so with whispered prayers for Joel's safety, I fell back to sleep.

I was not surprised to find out the next day that Joel had indeed been moved and likely in the middle of the night. Those first few days were a bit scary for me because I had no idea where Joel was, and he was not allowed to contact me. I lived with a strange mixture of confidence in my all-powerful, all-knowing Savior, along with anxiousness to hear from Joel.

I felt stretched to my limit and exhausted with the effort of just getting through the day. One moment, I would feel calm assurance, and the next I would feel like screaming out in rebellion against the whole situation. My emotions were a total roller coaster as I waited to hear from Joel. I could not imagine how either of us would handle a separation of thousands of miles if he were placed somewhere far away.

One evening after a few days of waiting and wondering where Joel was, I wrote this in my journal:

> Tonight my eyes are like faucets with no shutoff valve. I'm weary inside and out. I cry alone because I cannot cry with other people, but it is the most miserable, torturous kind of loneliness. I just can't seem to wrap my mind around five years of this. I don't want to live without Joel, but I can't just will myself dead. Oh God, comfort me with Your steadfast love. I know it never ceases; no,

and Your mercy is fresh every morning. Let me find strength in Your eternal kindness. Don't let me drown in my river of self-pity.

The desperation of my situation again threw me at the mercy of my Father. I knew I had no control over where Joel got placed. But I kept returning to the fact that God was in total control. I was learning so much about His sovereignty and resting in it. I was also learning how out of control I really was.

Days swept by without a word from Joel. I felt like I could really identify with the psalmist when he wrote, "If your instructions hadn't sustained me with joy, I would have died in my misery" (Psalms 119:92, NLT). During that waiting period, I wrote this poem of praise to God from the depth of my own neediness.

"Your Power in My Darkness"

So many unknowns,
Yet you know them all.
Please, Spirit, guide me,
Lest I slip and fall.
Darkness surrounds me,
Still I feel your guiding hand,
Showing me the path,
Helping me to stand.
My enemies assail me,
With doubts and fears.
But I hear you whisper gently,
"Fear not, I am here."

Tears fill my eyes,
Loneliness engulfs my being.
O lover of my soul,
Your power in me is so freeing.

Our Deepest Need

The story of Martha and Mary when their brother Lazarus died provided more insight for me in this area as well. They sent word to Jesus and expected that He would immediately come to them. Of course, a friend as dear as Lazarus would merit a speedy response by Jesus. But the Bible tells us that Jesus waited for two days before going to Bethany. By the time He went, He already knew that Lazarus had died. The Bible clearly states that Jesus loved this family. It was not a matter of His being too busy or caring more for Himself than for others. It is easy to judge Jesus's behavior according to human standards and expectations. But Jesus lived by a different set of expectations and standards. He lived with one overriding purpose: to glorify God by being in total submission to Him.

He reassured His disciples with these words: "Lazarus's sickness will not end in death. No, it happened for the glory of God so that the Son of God will receive glory from this" (John 11:4, NLT). He knew death would be a part of the equation, but it would not end there. God would be glorified in an ending that, while delayed, would be all the more powerful for the delay.

Of course, Jesus knew that Lazarus's sickness would not end in death, but Mary and Martha had no such reassurance. They waited with bated breath for Jesus to arrive on the scene and heal Lazarus before it was too late. And when He did not arrive in time, they were desolate.

When our feelings run haywire and we experience a depth of emotional pain that creates a physical ache within us, it is easy to desire nothing more than a relief from that pain. It is natural to alleviate the anguish, sometimes by ignoring it or by seeking diversions.

Mary and Martha found themselves in that place, longing for nothing more than to have their brother back and their pain allayed. When I read this story, I am struck by Martha's candid faith in the midst of her agony. Listen to her desperate trust in Christ as revealed in this conversation:

"Martha said to Jesus, 'Lord, if only you had been here, my brother would not have died. But even now I know that God will give you whatever you ask.'

"Jesus told her, 'Your brother will rise again.'

"'Yes,' Martha said, 'he will rise when everyone else rises, at the last day.'

"Jesus told her, 'I am the resurrection and the life. Anyone who believes in me will live, even after dying. Everyone who lives in me and believes in me will never ever die. Do you believe this, Martha?'

"'Yes, Lord,' she told him. 'I have always believed you are the Messiah, the Son of God, the one who has come into the world from God'" (John 11:21-27 fragmented; NLT).

Martha may have felt a sense of abandonment when Jesus did not rush on the scene and save the day. But when He did arrive, she did not seem to cling to that; rather, she threw herself at the mercy of her Savior, declaring her deep and abiding faith in the midst of the most horrendous of circumstances.

Since God is not always present with us in our suffering like we expect, we may feel like Mary and Martha, as though we are waiting in vain for Him to show up and perform some miracle to right the mess we find ourselves in. When He does not, it is easy to feel a sense of justification in attempting to arrange for our own comfort. I wanted so badly to be free of the pain of missing Joel and of not knowing what might be happening to him. I longed for anything to fill the ache of emptiness inside of me. But forcing myself to live in the agony with no anesthetic for the pain allowed me to anticipate God's hand with a greater expectation.

God is never too late, and His agenda does not run by our timetable. Jesus was purposeful in waiting until after Lazarus had died, and He told His disciples that this delay would be to God's glory. When we find our deepest longing is for God, and not for a quick fix, then we can begin to focus on His glory in the middle of our pain. Mary and Martha may have thought Jesus was too late, for He was too late to manage the situation according to their exceptions. His plans were so much bigger than anything they imagined. And because of God's immeasurable goodness in holding back, they were the recipients of a priceless gift: their brother brought back to life! Wow!

God's plans are so much vaster than our own. Through this period of so many unknowns as I waited to hear from Joel, He was showing me yet again that my deepest need was not a comfort for the pain. My deepest need was Him. Our family's deepest need was God. Even if the pain did not abate, knowing Him in a more personal way would bring incredible joy. God's plan does not always include a fix for our pain. But it always includes His glory and our enjoyment of Him. Two things we can wait for with eager expectation: God will glorify Himself, and He will draw us into a deeper enjoyment of Him, as we wait patiently for Him.

At times I could not even think straight to read God's Word. In those times, the Holy Spirit brought to mind verses I had memorized throughout my life. I remember as a little girl of six memorizing Scripture with my family. The first verse I recall committing to memory is: "I will go before thee and make the crooked places straight" (Isaiah 45:2a, KJV). Little did I imagine then what kind of crooked places I would find myself in later in life. But God knew, and He was going before me.

My heart sought after God with a new kind of desperation, not because I expected His comfort for my pain, but because I was beginning to realize how nothing else in life could truly satisfy my soul's longing.

Contact at Last

Early one evening as I sat in the backyard with my brother and his family who were visiting from Wisconsin, the phone rang. I had carried it with me faithfully for a week, hoping desperately to hear from Joel and terribly afraid of missing his call. Finally that call had come!

I listened to an automated message informing me that this call was from a federal prison inmate. Instantly I recoiled at the message. My mind rebelled! My husband was not a criminal! How could this be right? Nothing about my life made sense. My husband was an inmate at a federal prison! Even after living this nightmare for nearly two months, I could not accept, could not process, the idea of my dear Joel being a federal prisoner.

My eagerness to hear Joel's voice propelled me past the agony of yet another reminder of what he was in the public eye. I followed the instructions and punched "5" to accept the call.

"Hello, Sweets!" came Joel's charming voice!

"Hi!" I choked out. "Do you know where you are? Are you okay?"

I had so many questions, but many were immediately relieved by the tone of his voice. He was all right! And he was only a little over three hours away in Georgia at a facility in Jesup. The relief of knowing he was so close washed over me. While he was not at the closest facility, he was much nearer than I had feared. We could go see him! Our first conversation in over a week was awash with relief as Joel recounted to me the events of his travel from county jail, assuring me of God's protection and provision for each step of the way.

Joel's parents and I made immediate plans to visit him the next weekend. We had to send paperwork to the prison to be approved for visiting rights, so it took about ten days to get everything in order for us to go visit.

Joel could not wait for us to come see him. I wired him money, and he was able to set up an account for calling me. We were back in touch and could talk on the phone for about ten minutes a day. Joel only receives 300 minutes of phone time a month, which meant if we did not ration ourselves to ten minutes a day we would run out before the end of the month. Accepting this was really hard for me, but after so long with no contact, even a few minutes of conversation each day was a great relief.

Is It Worth It?

On July 19, nearly three weeks after Joel's middle-of-the-night transfer, we were able to go see him. That month felt like a year to me. I recorded this in my journal about our first visit:

> It was so wonderful and agonizing at the same time. To touch his face, kiss him, and see him hold the boys was so precious. But to know that long drives, security lines, and crowded visitor rooms with vending-machine food for lunch is to be our lot for the next few years was overwhelming. That is what we have to look forward to—week after week. Wow! How much we have lost. I'm so glad

we get to see him and spend time with him. But at the same time, I can numb the pain a little more when I'm not with him. I can almost pretend we have a normal life until I walk up to a concrete prison with double-razor wire fencing and go through metal detectors and X-ray machines just to see my husband for a few hours every couple weeks.

My emotions on the trip home were in an upheaval. Could I manage this kind of long day with three kids on a regular basis and every couple of weeks for the next few years? Was it worth it? Our time with Joel was so short compared to all the time it took to get there and return home. A twelve-hour day yielded a scant five hours with Joel, and in very restricted conditions.

My heart ached, not only because of the emotional stress of the day, but also from a sense of guilt for even wondering if visits were worth the amount of work they took. I could not imagine thinking Joel was not worth it and that our relationship was not worth it. But I questioned whether our relationship benefitted enough to offset the cost of the long, hard day.

As I looked into the future, I saw hundreds of Saturdays traveling back and forth, and I felt the weariness of every trip. I was crushed again by the realization that normal was a thing of the past. Our family would spend our free time driving and then waiting in line for our turn to visit Joel, instead of shopping with friends, going to soccer games, or hitting the beach.

Time was certainly not the only factor weighing on me. The cost of gas for each trip, not to mention eating vending-machine food at hugely inflated prices, was enough to make me want to gag. Where were we going to get the money to maintain a regular visiting schedule?

As we got closer and closer to home, my bone weariness gave way to a sense of immense loneliness. I was going to arrive home at suppertime with three hungry, tired, and dirty boys, and no one to help me to cope. I would unpack the car and put things away alone. I would bathe the baby alone. I would feed the kids and tuck Marshall and Jaden into bed alone, not just this time but over and over again, visit after visit, for years to come.

My focus was quickly turning inward and yielding a host of negative emotions. Stress was on the rise as I pondered our future.

I was learning again the important lesson of trust. When I imagined all that the future held and tried to figure out how we would handle it, I felt overwhelmed. But when I reflected on all that God had already done for our family and the ways He had provided for us up to that point, I found an amazing path of faithfulness. I am reminded of the words to an old chorus my mom used to sing to us when we were kids: "Oh, we've come this far by faith, leaning on the Lord, trusting in His Holy Word; He's never failed us yet."

God spoke into my bleak moments, "Have I ever not been enough for you? Have I let you down so far? Do you imagine that anything in your future is too hard for me to handle?"

So many times on this journey, I have wondered how I will ever manage one thing or another. As I look back, I honestly do not know how I have managed each thing. That is how God's grace works. We do not realize He is carrying us until we look back and see only one set of footprints in the sand.

The physical toll of our trips to visit Joel does wear on us. My van has had to have the transmission rebuilt, and we continue to pour on the miles. The travel does get costly. But again, I have found that something that seemed impossible to me reaps a harvest of joy for our family. We spend the time in the van on various activities, including homework and Bible study. We cherish each minute we get with Joel. And we work together to make each trip a special event. Our family has developed deep bonds through the time that we spend together. Is it worth it? Anything God asks us to do is worth it, simply for the joy of obeying Him, but we get to experience the added joy of deep growth in our family life as well.

THE REFINING PROCESS

God's Word likens the work of the Holy Spirit to affect change in a person's life to that of silver being purified. This picture has been explained and expounded upon many times. Recently a friend e-mailed me a short story referring to this picture. In the story, a woman went to visit a silversmith and asked him to explain the process by which the silver was purified. As he worked, he explained each step to her. When the woman asked how he knew that the silver was completely pure, he responded, "When I can see my reflection in it." The comparison is striking! Christ purifies us so that His image might reflect from us to a needy world. As we experience the purification process, it is easy to wrestle with the pain, to shy away from it, and to seek immediate relief. However, as Jesus holds us in the flame of intense trials, He is working in us to reflect His glory.

This comparison really struck a chord with me as I questioned what the impurities that are burned out of the silver represent in our lives. What are the things that Christ is stripping from us in order to present us pure and blameless before His Father? As I face the searing flames of trials in my own life, I wonder, What is Christ burning away?

Ignorance, Bras, and Christmas Gifts

One thing I see Christ dealing with in my own life is ignorance—an ignorance that resulted in judgment toward others. He is stripping away my preconceived ideas and teaching me truth in areas where I was previously unaware. A few weeks ago as I stood in line waiting to visit Joel, I began to chat with several of the others also waiting. As often happens when I get a chance to talk to other visitors, I found that they are facing similar struggles as I do and that they love an inmate fiercely enough to persevere, and that they are average working Americans trying to make sense of life. I felt a unique kinship with these people and a strange bond of identity as we all wrestled with issues related to an incarcerated family member. Christ whispered into my heart at that moment, "You were completely unaware of this hurting sector of the community before." I had to admit that the awareness I did have was a generic assumption that they had, at least to some degree, brought the suffering upon themselves.

As my ignorance has been swept away and replaced with not only awareness and sympathy, but also empathy, Christ has opened my heart and given me the desire to be a minister of His grace to these suffering people. Sometimes that simply means offering to hold a squirmy baby for a few minutes during the wait to get into the visitor room. Other times it has meant spending a portion of our visit time with Joel also visiting with another family in need of encouragement. On occasion it means participating in the financial needs of prison inmates and their families. Christ has purified my heart by removing ignorance and judgment and replacing it with awareness and grace.

My mother-in-law and I have learned so much through reading Carol Kent's books on her family's journey down the painful path of having their son incarcerated for life after being convicted of murder. In her book Between a Rock and a Grace Place, she tells the story of her husband's sensitivity to women in line at the prison who get turned away for wearing inappropriate clothing. After seeing their plight, he began to stash several black T-shirts in the trunk of his car to pass out when needed.[xii]

When my mother-in-law read this chapter, she resonated with its message. Many times as we have been in the process room waiting to visit Joel, we have watched someone set off the metal detector because they were wearing an underwire bra. (These are an official no-no at federal prisons.) We have observed, sometimes impatiently, as the person tries repeatedly to get through the metal detector, all the while unaware that it is her underclothing causing the problem. Finally, one of us has spoken up, suggesting that an underwire bra might be the culprit. This being discovered, the individual has been required to either remove the wires or leave and buy a suitable undergarment. We have watched the frustration of individuals losing precious visiting time with their loved one because they have to go purchase a new bra, and our hearts have gone out to them. Mom decided we would be ministers of God's grace by carrying extra bras in the trunk of our car to hand out when the need arises. Who would have thought we could share the love of God with needy people by carrying a few extra wireless bras with us! It is a rather strange thing to offer someone. Who wants to accept undergarments from a stranger in the parking lot of the prison? In any other setting, it would not only be inappropriate, but insulting. But at the prison, it is gratefully accepted. We are delighted at the little ways God is using us to spread His love.

On our second Christmas without Joel, God impressed on our hearts a desire to give extravagantly as an example of Christ's giving to us. One project He led us to was handing out presents in the parking lot of the prison after a visit. We went to see Joel on December 27, and when visiting hours were over, we made sure to be the first ones to leave the visiting area. We hightailed it to our van, where I had carefully stowed presents of Bibles, other Christian books, snacks, toys, and various treats. As people left the visitor area and headed to their cars, the boys passed out presents. It was such a joy to see the boys' delight in participating in this act of giving. They ran frantically to get another present from me each time they saw another person emerge from the visitor room. My one regret was that we did not have more people to help us pass out presents. We ended up missing some people, because we just could not catch everyone fast enough. Inside each adult gift bag was a letter I had written explaining God's gift to us and expressing my hope that each one would accept not only our present, but the gift of God's Son as well. What an incredible privilege to be used of God to show His love to these needy people. It was an opportunity I never would have had before, and it is one I am deeply thankful for.

Sin by Any Other Name

God has used this fiery trial to purify me of my own ignorance. He is also using it to purify me from sin.

Sin makes people uncomfortable. We would rather discuss our weaknesses, tendencies, or struggles. It is tough to name it and to call sin what it is: sin. We like to relieve our own sense of responsibility and guilt by giving rebellion against God a sanitized front. It sounds so holy and contrite to admit that I struggle with anger. But to say, "I chose to be angry and yelled at my children this morning, and that was sin," is so much harder. Recently I was listening to a message by Pete Briscoe in which he likened our concept of sin to Twinkies. He said we all know they are not good for our health, but one every now and then will not hurt, as long as we avoid a steady diet of them. Of course, his point was how counter-biblical that view of sin is. Sin is really more like cyanide. Every use is damaging in the extreme, because it is a poison that builds up in our system, becoming deadly. However, the primary problem with sin is not that it destroys us but that it eats away at God's glory. This refining process is teaching me to call sin in my life exactly what it is: an affront to a holy God.

God taught me so much about the sin of worry during the days of waiting to find out what would happen with Joel at his hearing. However, after Joel had been placed in Jesup, I began to get very used to hearing from him by phone every night. It was reassuring for me to know that every night he would call and give me a quick update on his day. I would know he was still healthy and safe and that he had not been falsely accused of something and thrown into the "hole."

One night in August, he did not call at the usual time. I waited with growing anxiety. Why wasn't he calling? What could keep him from the phone? Of course, I imagined every possible, morbid scenario, sure that something awful had happened. That evening I wrote a confession in my journal to God. I admitted my own dependence on outside circumstances to keep me comforted and reassured. I had allowed my sense of security to become wrapped up in phone calls from Joel and not in my Savior. This misplaced trust was sin.

When I finally heard from Joel, everything was fine, and there was a perfectly reasonable explanation for the delay. I shared with Joel my fear when he had not called. His response to me was precious, because it indicated that God was teaching him to trust in the right thing as well. "Tabitha, if something had happened to me and I couldn't call you, God would still be taking care of both of us. He would give us the strength to get through that too," he reassured me. And I knew he was right.

I still struggle with the sin of worry. I wonder what life will be like for us when Joel comes home, not because I do not long for his presence in our everyday life but because there will be many requirements of his probation that will make life different and difficult. I am concerned with how others will treat Joel and our entire family. And, of course, I wonder how we will make it financially. These concerns are all valid. But God's Word reminds us that worry cannot add even one hour to our day. So how could we expect to change things in the future by worrying?

One day my sister Dar Gail told me, "Worrying works. Ninety percent of the things I worry about never happen." I had to laugh. It is obvious that worrying has no bearing on whether something happens, but sometimes we feel as if it is our responsibility to worry. While we know that worrying does not affect any change on our circumstances, we fear that if we relax and something bad does happen, we will somehow be at fault for having done nothing. If I am not worried about our family, who will be?

On the other hand, Jesus says, "Therefore, do not worry saying, 'what shall we eat?' or 'what shall drink?'" (Matthew 6: 31, NKJV). Scripture is clear. If God tells us not to do something and we do it, it is sin. Worrying is a sin. It is not my responsibility to worry. It is my responsibility to trust and pray for God's wisdom.

Philippians 4:6 in the New Living Translation says, "Don't worry about anything. Instead, pray about everything. Tell God what you need and thank Him for all He has done." This verse not only tells us what not to do, but it clearly explains what to do. Pray about everything! Worrying is an affront to God's sovereignty, power, and loving kindness, because it is the opposite of prayerful trust. When I worry, I am essentially saying that God is not in control, is not powerful enough to take care of the situation, or does not love me enough to take care of me, none of which are remotely true. When I pray about everything, on the other hand, I am affirming that God is intimately involved in my life; He is infinitely good and sovereign; and He cares for me deeply. God is using this refining process to burn off the sin of worry and replace it with a trust that brings peace and rest.

Driven by Desperation

The psalmist cried out to God, "Before I was afflicted I went astray. But now I keep Your Word" (Psalms 119:67, NKJV). I can certainly identify with that statement. It was easy to wander before I found myself in this present affliction. Now my suffering renders me helpless and in a constant state of neediness before my Savior. The purification of suffering is not only burning away my sin, but it is also increasing my hunger for God and is making me more aware of His constant presence.

I think Ruth could identify with this kind of desperate hunger for God. In the tiny four-chapter book in the Old Testament, the story of God's incredible redemption unfolds. Ruth was from the land of Moab. She had married an Israelite man who had moved to Moab with his family because of a famine that was devastating Israel's food supply. But shortly after their marriage, he died. Ruth's father-in-law and brother-in-law also died, leaving her a sister-in-law from Moab and a foreign mother-in-law. Ruth had no hope of remarrying in that family. Both sons were dead, and to make matters worse, her father-in-law was gone too. Her hopes and dreams had been crushed. When her mother-in-law, Naomi, decided to return to Israel, Ruth said she would go with her. But Naomi objected. She felt that Ruth should stay in her own land and with her own people.

However, I believe Ruth had allowed the tragedy in her life to drive her to a point of hungering after God. He was using the great loss she suffered to draw her to Himself, for this was her response to

Naomi: "Don't ask me to leave you and turn back. Wherever you live, I will live, wherever you go, I will go. Your people will be my people. And your God will be my God" (Ruth 1: 16, NLT). Ruth forsook her old life, her homeland, and all the comforts it offered. She was that desperate for God.

A Holy Place

It was the week before Easter—our first Easter without Joel. I had planned to go visit Joel on the Saturday before Easter. This was to be my first visit without the kids. I thought wistfully of how nice it would be to share Communion as part of our Easter celebration on that visit. I quickly dismissed the idea, realizing how odd it would seem to Joel. He would not want to share Communion using juice and Cheez-It crackers from a vending machine in a room full of other people.

I was excited about the trip as I pondered all that I had been learning and looked forward to sharing with Joel without interruption. I was eager to hear what God had been teaching him too and was about to get a taste of it, even before my visit.

On Wednesday, Joel called, and we began talking about my visit. He informed me that one of his good friends whom he had been discipling would also be in the visit room with his wife and family. They wanted to spend some time with us during the visit. What he said next blew me away: "We want to get crackers out of the vending machine and share Communion together while you guys are here!"

I felt as if God was answering a prayer I had never prayed. I had been so sure Joel would think the whole idea silly that I had not even given it a second thought! I had to swallow back tears as I told him how the same idea had occurred to me a few days before, but I had brushed it off. Clearly God was working in both of us, giving us the passion and desire to be with Him in everything.

I cannot fully express the beauty of my drive up to Jesup that Saturday. This is how I described it in my journal:

> On the way up, I had a one-on-one worship service with God. It was so real, I felt as if Jesus were riding in the car with me. I listened to four messages and spent time in prayer, which really felt more like a visit with Jesus. Then I sang along with my new CD, at the top of my lungs, which is unusual since I am not gifted musically, to put it mildly. But I think God enjoyed it as much as I did. He doesn't seem to pay any attention to the sharp notes or the flat ones, for that matter. I really felt Him talking to me about relinquishing my future into His hands as I listened to "At Your Feet" (Casting Crowns). I want Him more than anything.

That Easter visit will stick out in my mind forever as a precious time of fellowship with my two best friends. Joel and I have both found ourselves intensely hungry for God in this time of separation from each other; and that hunger for God has drawn us closer to each other.

Later in my journal, I described our Communion service:

I was overcome by the change in Joel, the growth and depth, the dynamic aspect to his spirituality. He read the passage from Mark about Jesus's death and shared briefly how the soldiers mocking Jesus really made a mockery of themselves—just as we do every time we choose the way of sin. Then I recited the poem God had inspired me to write (I am so glad He also encouraged me to memorize it so that I could share it with Joel on our visit.) After that we passed around Cheez-It crackers and juice, gave thanks, and partook together. How powerful to celebrate our freedom in Christ together with Joel's friend and his family, right there in the middle of prison. Sure, we had to buy our Communion materials from a vending machine, and we had to share one cup (previously used for coffee); there was nothing orthodox or traditional about our gathering. But there was certainly something holy and precious.

My present pain makes me constantly aware of my own neediness. It intensifies my hunger for God. I cannot wait to know Him better. There is nothing more important than my Savior. Nothing satisfies like He does. I have found the psalmist's words in Psalm 119:92 and 143 to be so true: "If your instructions hadn't sustained me with joy, I would have died in my misery…As pressure and stress bear down on me, I find joy in your commands" (NLT).

Taking All the Time He Needs

The refining process takes time. That is why we call it a process. While we want to learn everything we can as quickly as we can, that is not usually possible. Humanly, we are restricted in our ability to process and assimilate. Furthermore, we are inhibited in our understanding and development by our raging emotions.

Joel recently commented in one of his letters to me: "I find it amazing that even still I am gaining new understanding and perspective on my behavior. I was so blinded and anesthetized by my sin that even when it came to light, I had trouble explaining or even comprehending it, much less understanding its far-reaching destruction in my life."[xiii]

When we experience severe physical pain, our minds can think of nothing else but the pain. There are moments, even hours, or possibly days that become a total haze because the pain is so all-encompassing. That does not mean healing is not taking place. The body goes to work right away to mend the brokenness. But the physical agony is so severe that we cannot appreciate the healing that is taking place.

I believe this is true emotionally as well. Many days the ragged agony I lived with was so overpowering that I could not think straight to accept or process any healing that was taking place. It was only much later, as I looked back, that I could see healing was indeed occurring, even in the darkest valleys I traveled.

Joel and I have often wondered, "How much longer, Lord? We cannot take this heat anymore."

However, the reality is that we are not only powerless to remove ourselves from the fire, but we are also incapable of assessing the success of the process. Only God can do that. When He gives us a glimpse of the work He is doing, like He did at our Easter service, we are overwhelmed by the beauty only He can produce.

As we look back over the past couple of years, we are both in awe of what God has taught us and continues to teach us. It seems like the more we learn, the more there is to learn, another one of God's amazing paradoxes.

A Lesson from Poppies

During World War I, a surgeon named John McCrae wrote a poem called, "In Flanders Field." This poem is a sad and beautiful description of the field of battle. The striking part of the description is that poppies were everywhere. These lovely flowers were blooming right in the midst of so much death and destruction, altering the landscape. This was not just the poet's imagination. Poppies were actually in bloom all over the fields. That is because poppies only flower when the soil is tilled. The seeds lie dormant until the ground is rooted up. Then they burst forth in striking color. What a picture of what God's grace can do in the rooted-up soil of our broken dreams.

The fires of purification are not comfortable. They are downright painful. There are moments, even whole days, when I feel like begging God to give me back my old life—the one where my husband and I lived together and shared everything; the one where we served God wholeheartedly on the mission field and felt the warm approval and support of our far-off loved ones; the one where we helped others in difficult circumstances, because we were so blessed; the one where my husband wrestled with the boys on the floor and read them bedtime stories; the one where we imagined ministering in far-off, exotic places, raising our kids in the jungle. That life was predictable. That life was safe. I loved God and wanted to serve Him in that life. I wanted our family to glorify Him in everything we did. But I wanted that to happen as a result of planning and dedication on our part, not through uncontrollable circumstances and bitter tragedy.

However, God had a different plan, and I am learning to believe it is a better plan. On the days when I long for my old life, God reminds me of the beauty He is building into my life and Joel's. He asks me if I would give back everything we have learned, everything we have experienced of Him, in order to go back to the old life. But most of all, He reminds me of the end product: purified till His image is clearly reflected.

GIVING OUT OF NEEDINESS

Lessons from my Childhood

One memory of God's provision from my childhood sticks out more than most. I was sixteen at the time, and even though I knew God provided for every detail of my family's life, this was the first time I saw Him providing for what I perceived to be more of an extravagance than a need.

We lived in the middle of the jungle. A trip to town was rare and costly. There were no roads. The only means of transportation was a small Cessna plane or a speed boat with a 65-horsepower outboard. Traveling by plane was costly. Traveling by river was time-consuming, uncomfortable, and potentially dangerous, since the trip took three to five days and entailed crossing two sets of rapids. It was our family's typical habit to make a trip to town once a year during the summer by plane. We would do any necessary doctor or dentist visits during that time, shop for school clothes and Christmas gifts, and generally enjoy city life for about ten days before returning to our jungle hermitage. Although we all loved our life in the jungle and generally disdained the social rigors of city life, we did look forward to our yearly visit to civilization. It was our only chance to shop in real stores, ride in cars, eat at restaurants, and watch television.

As missionaries we lived on an extremely tight budget, and by the time I was in high school, I had figured out that our family was on the poor end of even the missionary spectrum. We lived at the school base for missionaries' children, and my parents served as house parents for ten to twelve kids at a time, along with their own four. From a child's perspective, having money was not too important in that setting since there was rarely opportunity to use funds. We did not have a mall or restaurants, or theaters. Our basic necessities were covered, and entertainment consisted mainly of river sports and other outdoor activities.

Shortly before summer vacation, we began to plan our trip to town. One of the exciting parts of the plan was the arrangements we were making to rendezvous with friends who would also be out in town during the summer break. Joel and I had been dating for almost two years, and his family was one that we planned to meet up with while in town. I was excited about this because it would give our families a chance to get to know each other.

Our plans, however, were cut short one evening at dinner when Dad explained to all of us that we just did not have the money to get to town. We discussed going by river, but my mom in her wisdom cancelled that idea. Dad could not be away from his work long enough for us to spend three days each way on the river, anyway.

My older sister and I were convinced that God could and would provide for our trip, although we knew it was not a necessity. We announced to the family that we would be praying for God to make the necessary provisions for the trip. Then we started coming up with all kinds of ideas for making money. That was a bit tough, considering the limited market in our jungle village. The other people living there were either tribal people or other missionaries in about the same boat as we found ourselves financially. But we did manage to come up with a few successful ideas for raising funds. It was going rather slowly though, and summer was upon us. My parents tried to kindly help us understand and accept that we would not be going on a trip to town that summer. While we appreciated their concern that we deal with reality, Tammy and I felt a strange certainty that God was going to make a way for that trip to happen.

One day as we came in from swimming at the river, my mom urgently summoned us. We were nearly speechless when she shared with us the amazing story of God's provision. Someone had deposited sufficient funds into our missionary account in town to cover our trip! Mom was aghast at the gift. While Tammy and I were also euphoric, we were somewhat less surprised. It was not that we did not appreciate the gift; we did. It was just that we had been so confident that God was going to miraculously provide for this trip that our first reaction was to shout, "We knew it! We knew God was going to provide."

As it turns out, the gift had come from another missionary, equally as needy as we were, but with a generous heart and desire to serve God by sharing with others, even when it was sacrificial on their part. Their gift taught me immeasurable lessons about God's character and faithfulness. Their kind generosity toward our family showed me that God cares about the desires of our hearts. He loves to give us good gifts. He also delights to answer our prayers.

It is true that it is not God's main objective to be some cosmic vending machine that provides for our every whim; however, it is equally true that He is a good God who delights in giving His children good gifts. What those good gifts are, we must leave entirely in His hands. In this case, God gave my sister and me the faith to pray for a desire that He delighted to fulfill.

The example of generosity of this missionary to us has also challenged my thinking on the whole issue of giving. When we are in a financially, spiritually, or physically needy situation, it is easy to feel as though we have nothing to give and that we cannot share with others, because we are so needy ourselves. But this family's example to me has often reminded me that it is part of His plan to use us through giving, even when we ourselves are needy.

A couple of years ago, I read some statistics involving wealth around the world. I was challenged and a little surprised by these statistics: If you have any money at all in the bank and change lying around the house in a jar, or lost in couch cushions, you are among 8 percent of the wealthiest people in the world! Most Americans fit into that category. Even when our family struggles to make ends meet, we have a few quarters and pennies lying around the house!

This really hit home for me. My kids get three nutritious meals every day. They have clothes to wear to school that, while not necessarily the latest style, fit them and are not worn out or full of holes. We have a house that may be only 900 square feet, but it is enclosed and has appropriate climate-control devices. We have a vehicle that, although it requires routine fixes because of its age, still provides reasonable transportation for our family. We may be scraping the bottom financially according to the American standard of living, but we are still among the richest people in the world! That means we can still give. Often I have had the chance to remind my children that no matter how needy we are, there is always someone who is in greater need than us.

Obviously, giving is not just limited to financial resources, although that is what we immediately think of when we talk about giving. Beyond the material provisions we have, I find myself to be one of the wealthiest people in the world when it comes to family and wholesome relationships. I have parents, grandparents, siblings, in-laws, and even aunts and uncles who desire to participate in my life, assist me in my neediness, and encourage me to walk with God.

Recently my dad and I were discussing a frustrating situation regarding my present housing and whether I was going to need to move. I commented on the stress of moving alone, thinking of having to do this without Joel. My dad emphatically reminded me that if I move, I will not be alone. My family will rally around me, helping in any way they are physically capable. I will have emotional, physical, and spiritual support.

Far more important than material wealth or even the wealth of a strong family support system is the spiritual wealth we have in Christ Jesus. I am finding that no matter how needy we find ourselves in the material world, if we have Jesus, we are among the rich. Please do not misunderstand me; I do not mean to sound trite. I am not saying that physical needs are not real or that if we have Jesus, we just will not care about them. What I am saying is that many people around us have all their physical needs met and thus do not recognize their deepest need. They are blind to their own wretched poverty because of the veil of materialism. In places of extreme poverty around the world, the church often thrives. People are more in tune to their neediness, because of their physical conditions.

Paul says in 2 Corinthians 1:4: "He (God) comforts us in all our troubles so that we can comfort others" (NLT). Several years ago a movie was made called Pay It Forward. The basic point of the movie was that instead of paying someone back for a kindness, we should pass that kindness on to someone else. It was a secular movie, but the idea was biblical. God says that He comforts us so that we can pass it on to others. God teaches us, grows us, provides for us, and protects us, so that we will reflect His goodness to others by passing it on.

Jesus said in John 7:38, "Whoever believes in me...out of his heart will flow rivers of living water" (NKJV). In essence, Jesus fills us so He can spill out of our lives and into the lives around us. We are the conduit for God's love, grace, mercy, and care to flow to a needy world. When we receive from Christ and do not allow it to flow out of us, the life He pours into us becomes a cesspool of stagnation. Our attempts to absorb His love and grace for our own comfort and satisfaction result in decay. However, as we pass along His loving goodness, we experience the constant flow of living water through us. As believers, our wealth exists in knowing Christ, and the more we know Him, the more living water flows out of us to those around us.

The Needy Friend

Early in this trial, I felt the burden of being the needy friend and family member. My pride kept me from accepting the fact that I was going to need help and was going to be on the receiving end more than the giving end in many of my present relationships. It is often harder to be a receiver than a giver because of the pride that takes up residence in our hearts.

Ruth's example is noteworthy in this regard as well. She was a woman who lived in a very needy situation and was able to humbly accept the help of others. It must have been a real blow to her pride to have to go out into the fields of a stranger in a foreign land and glean the leftovers after the workers had come through and harvested the wheat. I cannot imagine the discomfort she must have felt that first day. She did not know anyone; she was unfamiliar with the culture, and she was reduced to the role of a working beggar. Scripture never indicates that she rebelled against this role. Rather, she humbly received the help Boaz offered, even the extra kindness he showed to her, with a heart of genuine gratitude.

God was working in my heart very early in this trial in the area of being a grateful receiver. My pride was being peeled away, and I was learning a lot about allowing others to minister to me in my neediness instead of always having to be the one to help others. As God worked in me to be a receiver, He showed me that being needy is not wrong, nor is it necessarily the result of laziness, poor planning, or foolishness. We all need one another. Sometimes we find ourselves in situations where that dependence is more acute.

I was in the process of accepting the role as receiver when God began to show me that we need not be solely one or the other—giver or receiver—but rather can be on both the giving and receiving end.

As I learned to receive, I did not lose the desire to give—to give back to those who were giving to me and to pass on to others who were also needy some of the kindness that was lavished on me. God is the author of generosity, and as He worked in my life, He challenged me to live a life of extravagant generosity toward those around me. Still, as much desire as I had to give, I had limited resources, not just financially, but also in the areas of time and energy.

A Different Way of Giving

One day my sister Tammy and I were talking on the phone about true friendship and the balance required in a good relationship. I expressed to her again my concern that my neediness would drain certain friendships of growth. The answer she gave me was a powerful kernel of truth: "Tabitha, when you walk with God, you naturally give back to the relationships you are involved in. By loving and clinging to Him in the middle of the dark valley you travel through, you are giving your friends insight into the faithfulness of God. You're giving the people around you the chance to see that God is true, and every promise He gives can be counted on. You give back by living a life of dependence. Your neediness is your gift."

Tammy's words were both a comfort and a rebuke. It was awe-inspiring for me to see that God was using me to give, without my being consciously involved. But it was also a chastisement of my own selfish pride. I was struck with my own desire to give as a means of making myself feel better. Giving is not primarily about us. It is about God. It is about reflecting His goodness to others. As I fretted over whether I was giving enough in my varying relationships with friends and relatives, I was actually looking inward. It was a self-absorption, not a God-absorption. God could and would use me to give, as I yielded to Him. The amazing part was that He was already using me in spite of myself.

What a miracle of God's goodness that in our neediness we can be givers! Ruth again provides us with a tangible example of this kind of giving. As she worked in Boaz's fields, she was invited to eat the noon meal with the other workers. Ruth gratefully accepted this kindness. At the end of the day, she returned to her mother-in-law, carrying with her not only the tremendous amount of grain she had gleaned but also the remainder of her lunch to share it. As she related the story of the day's events to her mother-in-law, Naomi responded, "God bless that Boaz! He's showing kindness to us as well as to our deceased family, by taking care of us."

Previously Naomi had been dubious about God's care for her or for their family. She did not seem to think that God was personally involved in their lives, except as a facilitator of tragedy. But when she heard Ruth's story of God's faithfulness and saw the bounty that Ruth brought to share with her, she began to see the kindness of the Lord and His blessing through this extended family.

That is not the end of the story. God continued to use Ruth not only in drawing Naomi back to Himself, but also in revealing His true nature and plan of redemption to the world. Not only did Ruth marry Boaz, thereby solving her family's immediate needs, but she became the mother of Obed, who was the grandfather of King David. This means Ruth became a direct ancestor of the Messiah. God gave Ruth the incredible privilege of being in the lineage of Christ! Because she was willing to be a conduit of God's grace to others, God used her in immeasurable ways to accomplish His plans.

When Jesus miraculously raised Lazarus from the dead, he came out of the tomb still wrapped in grave clothes. Jesus commanded those standing around to take off the grave clothes and set him free. Lazarus was at the mercy of the loved ones surrounding him. He needed help to remove the grave clothes. This is a beautiful picture of our needs within the body of Christ. Lazarus had to accept help to be set free. And Jesus told those around him to provide that help!

Receiving Through Giving

About a year after Joel had gone to prison, a family in our church faced a demoralizing situation in which they lost their ministry position. My heart went out to them as I saw all the pain they were facing, and I identified with its intensity. I began to pray that God would show me how to share in their suffering. Their plight was much different from mine, but many of the elements were the same. The family suddenly found themselves without a livelihood and faced a difficult move across the country for logistical reasons. As I prayed for them, God challenged me to participate in their sufferings by sharing financially in the cost of their move. At first this idea seemed absurd. After all, I am living on a single income, raising three kids and supporting an incarcerated husband. It is not like I have unlimited resources. God gave me a specific amount He wanted me to give. I knew I had that much in my bank account, but I was tempted to check out all my upcoming expenses and balance my books before I obeyed. God would not let me. He impressed upon my heart the importance of obeying Him without question.

"Oh, Lord!" I responded. "But you're asking me to give so much!"

"My dear child, listen to me! You are the receiver today. You are not the giver," I heard Him reply.

I cannot explain how God's economy works. I only know that as I obeyed Him and relinquished my "right" to hold on to material wealth, I became the receiver. I gave the finances God had given me to this needy family, and I was merely the conduit. God could have provided for them some other way, but He chose to use me. He gave me the blessed privilege of being His avenue to taking care of them. God gifted me with the opportunity to play a part in His body and to comfort others even as I had been comforted. What a joy there is in knowing that as receivers, we can also be givers, and as givers, we will invariably be the receivers. This is one of God's great paradoxes.

VASES AND STAINED GLASS WINDOWS

Recently I thought of a word picture that describes our life quite well. Our life was like a glass vase. It was large, becoming, and multicolored. It was useful. It was admired by some. It was ignored by others as just another vase. But it fulfilled its purpose. Then the vase was placed on the anvil of trial and crushed with the hammer of tragedy. The pieces shattered, with shards flying in every direction. The brokenness could clearly not be repaired. The vase was no more. It could never be again. At first, it seemed as though the destruction was so complete that not only was the vase no more, but even the pieces were nothing but useless, jagged remains.

Then something mysterious, even miraculous, began to happen. God, in His gentle, almost imperceptible way, began to pick up the pieces: the tiny, jagged shards and the larger ones with misshapen edges and random cracks. It was not clear what He intended to do with so much "trash," but slowly something began to take shape. He was not putting back together the vase; He was building something different—a stained glass window. Each piece of brokenness began to come together to make something beautiful.

Our life will never look like it did. But God is a master designer, and He loves to build beauty into our brokenness. That is what He is doing in us and for us. What He is creating is new, and as I look at it, I see new rays of His talent and His gifts reflected in our broken pieces.

Learning New Things about Ourselves

We are learning things about ourselves that we had overlooked or simply not discovered before. Even if the design that is taking shape under the Master's hands is ultimately intricate and beautiful, the process is often in direct contrast. On the other hand, some of the discoveries bring us new joys.

One such discovery for Joel is his artistic talent. Shortly after moving to Jesup, Joel began taking a drawing class simply to pass the time. He was surprised when the teacher complimented his work and suggested that he had natural talent. But he did discover quickly that he enjoyed the learning process. Joel found that he was a quick study, and shortly after his drawing class began a painting class. That too, he found, came easily for him. It has been an interesting and exciting journey for Joel in discovering this hidden talent. He has already had several chances to share his talent with others. He has drawn pictures for inmates to send home to their families, and he has sent us a couple presents as well. His first painting hangs on the wall in our living room, a constant reminder of the Master Artist's work in our lives.

I have not discovered any hidden talents of my own. However, one piece of multicolored glass that God has brought out in my life is the desire to share my story. I remember so well the first few days and weeks after we were informed of the investigation.

I dreaded the looks I would get. I feared telling my family and friends the sordid story. I hated the infamy. I felt an overwhelming sense of dread that this was to be the story of my life.

About a year after Joel had been incarcerated, a friend of mine from a church in Wisconsin asked if I would share my story with the ladies' groups in her church. This was a church Joel and I had been involved in years ago when we were in missions' training. They had supported us during our time of service in Venezuela. When I began working with Wycliffe Associates after Joel had gone to prison, they immediately joined me in financial partnership. So we had a long history with this church. But since it is in Wisconsin, there are only a handful of people that we know personally in the church.

This was the first time anyone had asked me if I would be willing to share my story. I knew the time had come to begin telling others of God's faithfulness in our lives. What was surprising though was that I felt eager to share, even though I labored over exactly what to share and how to share it. I wanted so badly for people to see God's hand in our story and to know that He is the one deserving of recognition. I longed for the psalmist's words to be true of our family: "They will see in our history the faithful love of the Lord" (Ps. 107:43, NLT). God had worked so many miracles in the scattered, broken pieces of my life that sharing my story has become a joy to me.

Authenticity is a powerful tool in the hands of God. So many times we want to cover our tracks, hide the gruesome details of our journey, and glaze over our issues. In many ways, the option to hide the repulsive nature of our tragedy was stripped away from us. But we could have begun "Operation Damage Control" and salvaged a vestige of dignity. We could have mustered our courage and covered our roiling emotions. Frankly, that is what we sometimes did. But God would not let us live out "Operation Damage Control" as a lifestyle. He was working in us to be authentic, to accept the pain as part of the process, and to avoid the human desire to run and take cover. There are certainly people who are repulsed by our story, but no one who hears our story and sees what God is doing in us can deny His power. It is clearly not us, nor is it our story that is attractive. What is attractive is God's amazing grace.

God has taken a vase and transformed it into a stained glass window that is really rather dull, until the light of His glory shines through it. Then the patterns refract and titillate, scattering light in every direction.

A Trust That Keeps on Growing

Trusting God over the long haul requires believing that He is good and that He does only good. He is not in the business of grudgingly taking care of us. Nor does He have good intentions but get busy elsewhere and forget about us. Trust also requires that we believe He is sovereign and powerful. A wimpy God will do us no good.

Scripture is clear that God is both powerful and good. We have to come to a point where we believe that, no matter what evidence there appears to be to the contrary. No matter what happens in this life, God is good, and He is doing something good in us.

I think about all the examples in Hebrews 11, the great "Hall of Faith" chapter. So many of the people described in that chapter died without seeing the promises of God fulfilled. But they are in that chapter because they died believing God anyway. They trusted Him even when things became increasingly worse.

In our journey, some things have gotten worse. Some difficulties have intensified. Nothing about living alone and raising three boys without their father present in the home could be categorized as easy. And daily I am aware that the other shoe could drop. Things could get even worse. Car accidents and cancer diagnoses are happening all around us. What if that happens to us?

The fear that one of us might die while Joel is in prison haunted me for several months after he was incarcerated. On New Year's Eve night, the first year Joel was gone, I was involved in a disaster that could have ended in utter tragedy.

New Year's Eve was spent celebrating with family at my sister Tammy's house. In the wee hours of New Year's morning, 1:30 to be exact, I headed home with my three drowsy children tucked carefully into my already-full van. Dar Gail, my younger sister, was to follow and catch up with me at home to help with putting the kids to bed.

In Tammy's yard is a small pond, just beyond the driveway surrounded by young palm trees—more like bushes at this stage. Since winter is particularly dry in Florida, the receded water level had left a steep bank of about three to four feet.

As I pulled away from Tammy's yard, I remembered a bag of items I had left behind in her dining room. Of course, being overtired and not thinking very clearly, I decided to back up to the house and retrieve the items.

Although I could clearly see their house behind me, I misjudged my direction and the angle of my tires on the driveway. Before I knew it, I felt the brush of palm fronds against my bumper. Of course, I put the brakes on immediately, chastising myself for running into one of my brother-in-law, Larry's small palms. As I braked, we slid, and the next thing I knew, we were at a sharp angle on the bank of the pond, leaning precariously toward the water — Roman and I on the leaning side, and Marshall and Jaden on the high side.

At first, I was unsure how close to the water I was and if I was just sinking in mud or about to fall sideways into the pond. While the pond is not deep, still it was about five to seven feet, sufficient to immerse the van. I knew if we fell in, there would be precious few moments in utter darkness and confusion to unlatch the baby and get him out, as well as help the other two to the surface. Of course, there was the danger of the van landing in such a way as to pin one or more of us down. I processed the situation quickly and realized I had no time to waste. Marshall asked if he should exit the car, since he was on the high side, but as soon as I told him to, I changed my mind and explained quickly that he needed to stay where he was, because I needed all the weight possible on that side of the van in order to keep it from tipping into the water. Of course, I also feared the jolt of the door would be just enough to send the van sliding into the water. I began to frantically call my sister's cell phone, which she did not answer.

Jaden offered to pray, which he and Marshall did loudly amid crying. Marshall and I both rolled down our windows, and the boys unbuckled themselves, but we left the baby buckled. When no one answered the phone, Marshall suggested I honk the horn. Great idea, Marshall—why didn't I think of that?

So between honking the horn and calling, someone finally came out of the house and discovered our dangerous predicament.

My dad, mom, and both sisters ran frantically to help. They furiously levied weight on the high side of the van and pulled the children out. By God's grace, I was able to reach behind me and with one smooth click of each buckle, release the baby. I then grabbed him by one arm, due to my awkward angle, and dragged/tossed him into the waiting arms of my mom and sister.

Larry, who had been sleeping, was desperately summoned, and he rushed out to get his truck and a chain in an attempt to stop the van from going the rest of the way into the water. Once the children were out, my dad and mom screamed for me to crawl out. It was then I realized how much of a panic mode I was in. I could not move. It took a moment to mentally assess the situation, force my muscles to relax, and struggle up and out the open passenger door. The whole fiasco had lasted less than twenty minutes, but the trauma was enough to send us reeling for hours!

We have discussed this near tragedy over and over as a family and have come back again and again to God's grace in panicky situations! He is never taken by surprise, and His faithful, steadying hand was evident again in our lives.

Still, I could not help but wonder what I would have done if one of us had not made it out safely. What if the unthinkable had happened and the car had tipped into the pond, and I could not get all three of my children and myself out safely? How would I have gotten word to Joel? How would we have processed and grieved and shared in one another's pain with the miles that separate us?

I am so grateful that in this case, we had the best possible outcome, but we know and have come to rest in the assurance that regardless of the outcome, He is sufficient! It comes down to this simple truth: if God is good and does only good, then I can trust Him with every "what if" in our future. When I am sold out on the truth that God is powerful and He is on my side, I can lay all my concerns for our future at His feet. "Though He slay me, yet will I trust him" (Job 13:15, NKJV).

Horatio Safford did face the crippling loss of his children while separated from his wife. He was not spared such grief. And yet, he allowed God to use it to drive him closer to his Savior. I can see by the light of such historical testimonies that God's grace is indeed sufficient and will be sufficient for our family as well.

As I write this, I am still more than three years away from having my dearest love home with me. We have a long road ahead of us. When I think about trusting God with the long haul, I realize that I am on the short end. I have a ways to go. I identify with the saying, "All I have seen teaches me to trust the Creator for all I have not seen." Trusting God is being built into each step Joel and I take on this journey.

Hope Deferred

Joel has worked very hard to get into a program in prison that is related to addictions. The entry process is very difficult because one of the benefits of the program is a year reduction on his sentence. After much work to put the right paperwork in place, Joel was accepted into the program and then waited nearly six months to begin the classes. During his first month of class, we began to research the requirements for his getting the year off. Of course, when he was accepted into the program, we got very excited that his time in prison would be cut down by a year.

Unfortunately, because of specific stipulations for the state of Florida, it now appears that Joel is unlikely to get time off for taking this program. We had made a conscious attempt not to get our hopes up for this time off. But that was nearly impossible. For the last eighteen months, the carrot of a year off has been dangled before our noses. Now the carrot has suddenly been retracted with no recourse! It is disheartening, to say the least. I feel an overwhelming sense of loss and frustration. Why did we put so much energy and hope into this for it to fail? Even though I know it is part of God's plan for good in our lives, at the moment it feels incredibly wrong. Proverbs 13:12 says, "Hope deferred makes the heart sick" (NLT). My heart truly feels sick as I absorb this recent news.

I beg God for respite. I wrestle with my present circumstances and the seeming endlessness of the course before us. Sometimes I think, I just can not do this for three more years. In those moments God reminds me, "I will never ask you to go somewhere that I do not go with you. I am enough for you." Trusting God means taking life moment by moment and believing God for that moment.

I used to say that God never gives us more than we can handle, and I meant that He would help us through anything that comes our way. Now I am convinced that God constantly allows more than we can handle to come into our lives, to throw us at His mercy, and to turn us to Him for strength and comfort.

As I shared with one of my friends the struggle I was facing with accepting the news that Joel would not be getting the year off, she reminded me of God's eternal goodness and His desire for only good for us. She pointed out that God will not allow our family to be separated for any longer than is absolutely necessary for our good. God's desire is not for our harm, and it is not for our demise. On the contrary, it is for our good. It took much effort and many prayers to get Joel into this program. If it was not for the time off, then God answered those prayers for some other purpose.

We knew that Joel could benefit from the tools offered in this course. And we prayed that he would. Now God is allowing him to focus on that process and grow where he needs to, instead of focusing on doing it all right in order to merit the year off.

Sometimes when God answers our prayers with a "yes," we become certain of the path that lies ahead. We are confident that He answered "yes" for some specific purpose. In this case, we thought the purpose would be to shorten Joel's sentence. But again, we have been reminded that He is in control, and His ways are not our ways. Shortening Joel's sentence is certainly a normal and good desire on our part. But God has reminded us again that the single best desire we can have is for Him. When our desire is for God, our trust in Him grows. We can look at our situation and rest, knowing that God is working for our good. That is nothing short of miraculous.

So often our lives are wasted moment by moment as we pursue lesser gods. Joel and I are learning through the intense fire of suffering not to waste even one minute on a lesser pursuit. That means that even when we seek something good, asking God for His blessing, we seek it with open hands, not allowing it to hinder our ultimate pursuit of God. So when our hope is deferred, it is deferred right back to God.

Every circumstance we find ourselves in will not always feel good. God does not promise us sunshine and rainbows. We cannot define and demand the kind of good we want. Trusting God means believing that He knows best, and the good that He plans is indeed the highest good. The process might take us through dark valleys, but the promise is that no dark valley will be traveled alone, nor will it be useless. Each dark valley will draw us into a deeper place of safety in His arms. Martin Luther put it this way, "Oh! His grace and goodness toward us is so immeasurably great, that without great assaults and trials, it cannot be understood." The trials we face are the platform God uses to display His grace and goodness.

God Is Pleased with Me

In the beginning of this painful journey, I would have proclaimed that I did not want to waste a moment of the pain. I remember wanting so badly for God to be pleased with my response to the pain. I felt like saying, "Is this pleasing to you, God? If not, then what?" (I did not intend to be proud, but looking back, I see it as a kind of sneaky pride that led me to believe that I had it in me to respond properly and show God what a good Christian I was.) Although I knew that God is pleased with us perfectly in His Son and that my trial was not a test for me to pass, I could not help treating it like that. I wanted to learn what God had for me, and I wanted to be in a place of maturity in my spiritual life. I did not want my suffering to be wasted. Somehow I imagined that making good use of my pain would mitigate the suffering.

Slowly God began to change my heart as I became increasingly aware of His sovereignty in my situation and my own helplessness. I realized how little control I have, not only of my present circumstance, but even of my own reactions and attitudes. I also began to accept that I have no control over the length or depth of this valley, and while Christ is the only possible mitigation for my suffering, He is not some prescription to be taken twice daily. Total abandon and reliance on Him is my only recourse.

Now, my question to God is, "Is this glorifying to you?" And I mean it, not so He will be happy with me, but so others will see that He is truly worthy. It may seem like a subtle change, but it has been tremendously freeing. God is pleased with me because I am in Christ. And He is glorified when I rest in that truth and allow this trial to make me more dependent on Him. By my utter dependence on Him, I show Him to be what He is—faithful, loving, and completely in control.

Before, I wanted God to show me each step, and I wanted to successfully follow Him, much like a person who is learning a new skill. A young bride-to-be may work very hard to learn all the dance steps before her big day. But when she dances with her father, the dance is truly beautiful, because she is following his lead. She is so in tune to him, as her loving and supportive father, that they sway effortlessly in time to the music, unaware of outside factors and unencumbered by patterns, steps, or the rules of rhythm. Similarly, I am becoming aware of His lead and can sway to the music of each new pattern in our lives, thereby not wasting one moment of time with Him.

God's goodness is the framework that holds the stained glass pieces together in the beautiful window that He is building out of the brokenness that is our life. God has put the framework in place, and my trust in Him allows each piece to fit together perfectly. What beauty God brings from unthinkable sorrow!

LOOKING FORWARD

A Picture Worth a Thousand Words

Joel and I did not have a typical dating relationship for a number of reasons, not the least of which was our physical location. One of our most memorable dates was an adventurous day trip of hiking through the jungle and climbing a set of huge waterfalls. My sister Tammy and her fiancé, Larry, went with us.

The waterfall was located outside the valley where Joel and his family lived, so he had climbed it and hiked around it many times with his brothers. The climb took about two hours and was filled with treacherous jumps, slippery rock overhangs, and steep inclines. There was no path. But Joel was quite comfortable forging a way. We doggedly followed him, confident of his ability to lead us to the top. Although the climb was exhausting, we were young, and an occasional glimpse of the valley below through the thick foliage captivated us. I knew we were making some dangerous jumps, but it never occurred to me that we were taking unnecessary risks. It just did not seem risky with Joel as our guide.

By the time we reached our destination, a level spot that opened up to a gorgeous view of the waterfall on one side and the jungle valley below, we felt spent but completely gratified. Hot and sweaty, we found a small enclosure of rocks that led to a swimming hole—a part of the waterfall that had taken a detour and filled up a natural cavern in the huge rocks. It was like a Jacuzzi because the water was swirling around so much. It was cool and refreshing after our long hike.

Larry had been the only one brave enough or smart enough to carry a camera with him, so I have him to thank for one of my favorite snapshots ever taken. He captured a shot of me as I came up out of the water with my eyes still closed. I look far from stunning; what makes the picture such a treasure is Joel in the background. He has a look of complete adoration and contentment on his face, with his eyes fully focused on me! As his girlfriend, I guess I knew that he looked at me in a special way, but actually seeing it captured in a snapshot was very striking. Every time I look at that picture, I am reminded of how Joel sees me.

It is easy to focus on the negatives in life. It seems to come naturally to the human heart. When I found out about Joel's hidden life of sin, I was understandably devastated, and I wondered if he really loved me. How could someone love me and hurt me that much? Of course, Joel insisted that his own stupidity led him down that path and that he had always loved me.

Recently in a long visit we had, Joel said to me with tears in his eyes, "The truth is I loved my sin more than my wife. That was the truth. I wouldn't have seen it that way. I wouldn't have known that myself at the time. But that is the truth. And really, I loved my sin more than my Savior."

This kind of candid conversation marks our relationship these days. We may go weeks between visits, but we are closer now than we have ever been in our lives. And there was a time when I could not imagine that. I thought we had it all. I thought we were blissfully happy. I thought we knew each other so well, supported each other so fervently, and loved so deeply. I cannot wait to see what our love is going to look like in the coming years.

Our Love Affair with Sin

Joel's open confession to the truth of his love affair with sin convicts me of my own love affair with sin. How many times have I lived in a way that says I love my sin more than I love my Savior? The fact is, every time we choose to be angry and lash out with ugly words, every time we have a bad attitude, every time we gossip, and every time we complain, we are loving our sin more than we love our Savior.

Last summer I read the Narnia series to my boys for family recreation time. In The Voyage of the Dawn Treader, there is a scene in which Aslan has to remove the dragon scales from one of the children who has been turned into a dragon in order to return him to human form. The boy/dragon has tried repeatedly to remove the scales himself, but they keep coming back as instantly as he removes them. When Aslan removes them for him, it hurts. But it is a therapeutic kind of pain and presently begins to feel good as he realizes he is human again! I asked Marshall, then twelve, why it hurt when Aslan removed the scales. With insight beyond his years, he replied, "Because we love our sin too much." Sin is a disease whose worst symptom is numbness.

One of the striking points of the word picture is that it is fruitless to attempt removal of those scales ourselves. Joel had tried so many times to quit his sinful and even criminal patterns of behavior. And he had even felt moderately successful at times. But that success never lasted. Each of us knows the feelings of trying and failing repeatedly. But when we allow God to remove those scales, they are truly removed.

Joel shared with me that he had repeatedly begged God to take away his sinful obsessions. He said, "I really thought I wanted to be free of them. I didn't. It was like holding something in my hands and asking God to take it from me, but every time He would tug at it, I would close my grip and hold on tighter. I asked Him to take it, but I didn't really mean it. God does not force us to give up our sins. But He does lovingly drive us to a place of yielding to Him." The blessing of consequences, coupled with truth and brokenness, has led Joel to that place of really letting God take control of his life and desires.

Anticipation in Christ

As we look into the future, we tremble with anticipation and fear. Joel has three more years to serve in prison. We visit regularly and do our best to keep him involved in the children's lives. But we both cry when we think of how much he is missing of each of their lives. Roman, who was not even walking when he went to prison, will be in kindergarten when he gets home. What will Roman think of having his daddy actually in the home again? Marshall, who was in grade school, will have his driver's permit.

And Jaden will be in middle school already! It is hard to watch them grow up without Joel around. We struggle with accepting the lost time.

Furthermore, Joel was given a life sentence of probation, which means when he does come home, he will have to follow specific guidelines and report to a probation officer on a regular basis for the rest of his life. Additionally in the state of Florida, he will be placed on the sex offender list and never removed. For the rest of our lives, he will be looked on as suspect. While our dream is to move beyond this phase in our lives, in many ways, that will be impossible because of the stipulations set on us by his sentence. This is scary and even frustrating. We wonder how we will handle the invasive nature of probation. How will we live gracefully with the brand of a scarlet letter?

So much of our future is undeniably altered. We are painfully aware of how difficult it will be for Joel to get a job. It is also sobering to realize that he may not be allowed to attend his own children's school programs and other activities. We have so many unknowns to face, and much of it looks very daunting.

As children, when we did something wrong, we learned to say "sorry" very quickly in the hopes of avoiding consequences. As adults, we still tend to feel that once we are regretful of our actions and have changed our attitude, the consequences ought to abate. Recently Joel shared with me how easy it is to become resentful. Even as he knows that his own crime produced our present circumstances, there is an inner voice that keeps crying, "I said I was sorry."

"But," he went on to express, "the real truth is no matter how sorry I am, I have two choices: accept and own the consequences, asking God to give me the grace to live within their bounds, or become bitter and resentful, fighting against every infringement that I gauge to be unfair."

"Sorry" does not magically erase the past. It cannot undo the damage and right the wrongs. True repentance understands and accepts those limitations. Joel is learning that owning his consequences is one way he can honor God. He lives out repentance by accepting stipulations and requirements that may seem excessively severe.

God has also given Joel the grace to accept even the typical discomforts he experiences in prison as platforms for God to work in his life. As I pondered sharing our story in this book, I asked Joel to write a description of some of the difficulties of prison life and then tell me how God was using them to grow him up in Christ. Here is what he wrote:

> I am reticent to describe the difficulties of prison life, although it is a very difficult, degrading experience. I feel that for me to express the indignities I am forced to endure is quite irrelevant. What I will say is this: I am to blame for my suffering. It is a daily reminder of my sin.

> I slip occasionally into self-pity and resentment for the severity of my sentence, which includes not only my prison term but also a life sentence of probation with very extensive restrictions. But I keep coming back to the inexorable truth that no matter what happens

to me, God is in control. He knows my sufferings. He is not unaware of my pain. He has a plan to use my sufferings to produce in me a vessel of His grace and love.

I also feel that any description of my conditions in prison would only serve to detract from the real tragedy: the undeserved suffering I have caused for those whom I love—most of all my Savior.

If this story has a villain, I am he. Perhaps all the reader of any story desires is for the villain to suffer. Of course, there are those rare stories in which the villain has a change of heart and is redeemed. That is truly what has happened to me. I deserve to suffer exactly what I am going through right now. In all actuality, I deserve to suffer more. I deserve hell. But Christ has redeemed me, and He didn't stop this rescue mission when my future was secured in heaven. Instead He is working through every situation I face here on earth to change my heart and make me into a vessel that reflects His image to the world around me.

Even as we know that our road ahead will not be easy, we find ourselves anticipating God's amazing work through the difficult times. It is a strange kind of excitement that wells up inside of us as we look back over the past couple of years and see all the changes He has made in our lives. It was not a path I would have chosen for us, but neither could I have known the incredible work He would do in Joel's heart or mine along that path.

Nothing about our future resembles what I expected for our lives. But just like God was giving Job a gift, Joel and I have both come to believe that God has given us a gift, the gift of Himself, the gift of knowing Him better and loving Him more, the gift of living out His grace and forgiveness, and the gift of seeing Him face-to-face.

A NOTE FROM THE AUTHOR

If I have one concern for this book, it would be that some might misunderstand my intentions. I in no way want to imply that my handling of pain is the only sound method for development and growth through tragedy. Nor do I want to suggest that I have handled our suffering in an exemplary manner. Much of what I share in this story relates to what I have learned through this deep valley I now walk. But much of it has taken a great amount of time to absorb and process. It is not a matter of an assembly-line system that results in a desired product. Rather, each facet of the anguish I have experienced took tremendous time to process, and the pieces did not always seem to fit together into what has become the mosaic of God's grace in our lives. Sometimes I felt like I was learning the same things over and over again, only to find myself back at the beginning. There is no one time-tested method for handling the agonies we face in life. Each one's suffering carries with it a different dynamic.

However, what is true in every case is that "God is good and does only good" (paraphrased from Psalms 119:68). If you are going through your dark valley right now as you read this book, please remember this one thing: While no amount of handling the pain will guarantee results, "God is good and does only good."

Writing our story has not mitigated the suffering I experience, but in some ways it has proved to be therapeutic. It has forced me to stop and recognize the patterns of God's work in our lives. It has allowed me to take the time I needed to process our experiences. It has challenged me to live with one compelling purpose, the glory of my Savior. And it has offered me the opportunity to live out His goodness and grace before others.

The title of this book stems from one of the biggest lessons I have learned so far on this journey. We may think that joy can only come when the sorrow has passed. But the truth is that many times, the joy actually comes in the mourning.

ENDNOTES

i. Larkin, Nate. Samson and the Pirate Monks. Nashville: Tommy Nelson, 2006

ii. Sittser, Jerry W. A Grace Disguised. Grand Rapids: Zondervan, 1995

iii. Kent, Carol. A New Kind of Normal. Nashville: Thomas Nelson, 2004

iv. Price, Joel. Journal Entry. September 2009

v. Ten Boom, Corrie. I'm Still Learning to Forgive. Carmel. Guidepost Associates, Inc. 1972

vi. Price, Joel. "Untrustworthy." essay. October 2010

vii. Chambers, Oswald. My Utmost for His Highest. Grand Rapids: Oswald Chambers Publications, assoc. 1992

viii. Piper, John. Don't Waste Your Life. Wheaton: Crossway. 2007

ix. Price, Joel. Personal letter. June 2009

x. Briscoe, Pete. Message. Tellingthetruth.com

xi. Crabb, Larry. Shattered Dreams. Colorado Springs: WaterBrooke Press. 2001

xii. Kent, Carol. Between a Rock and A Grace Place. Grand Rapids: Zondervan. 2010

xiii. Price, Joel. Personal Letter. March 2010

The Prices

Please pray for:
Tabitha Price
MAST Theory Coordinator
Wycliffe Associates
www.tabithaprice.com
www.wycliffeassociates.com
tabitha_price@wycliffe
associates.org
(407) 312-7406
2856 N. 83rd St.
Milwaukee, WI 53222

Jaden

Tabitha

Roman

Joel

Marshall